AMERICA'S SHAME

AMERICA'S SHAME

Women and Children in Shelter and the Degradation of Family Roles

Barbara A. Arrighi

Westport, Connecticut
London

Library of Congress Cataloging-in-Publication Data

Arrighi, Barbara A.
   America's shame : women and children in shelter and the
degradation of family roles / Barbara A. Arrighi.
      p.   cm.
   Includes bibliographical references and index.
   ISBN 0–275–95732–2 (alk. paper)
      1. Shelters for the homeless—Kentucky—Case studies.   2. Homeless
women—Kentucky—Case studies.   3. Homeless children—Kentucky—Case
studies.   4. Poor women—Kentucky—Case studies.   5. Poor children—
Kentucky—Case studies.   6. Family policy—United States.
   I. Title.
HV4506.K4A77   1997
362.83′83—dc21   96–47614

British Library Cataloguing in Publication Data is available.

Library of Congress Catalog Card Number: 96–47614
ISBN: 0–275–95732–2

First published in 1997

Praeger Publishers, 88 Post Road West, Westport, CT 06881
An imprint of Greenwood Publishing Group, Inc.

Printed in the United States of America

The paper used in this book complies with the
Permanent Paper Standard issued by the National
Information Standards Organization (Z39.48–1984).

10 9 8 7 6 5 4 3 2 1

Contents

Part III. Solutions: Some Old, Some New

Tables

Preface

This book is written with what Max Weber called *verstehen*; that is, with a Weberian understanding or empathy, especially for children living in poverty. It is written for children who live in unstable economic circumstances and cannot rely on overwhelmed parents for physical safety and emotional security. It is written for children who cannot trust a system that declares the family to be sacrosanct and yet continues to erode efforts to save children. Children are betrayed twice in this society—first by their primary caretakers and then by policy makers. Despite an emerging consciousness that children whose primary needs go unmet are likely to repeat the cycle of poverty, societal responses to the children are becoming weaker. Yet what happens to poor children eventually affects all children.

Nowhere in this book will the reader find the word *homeless* (except in works cited). The term denies collective responsibility for the lack of affordable housing and for the lack of employment that pays sufficiently for a family to afford housing. If I could hope to accomplish one thing with this book, it would be to abolish the classification or labeling as *homeless* of those who are without homes. The use of labels depersonalizes a heterogeneous population and falsely exonerates society. To use a well-worn sociological phrase, it "blames the victim."

Although the information about poverty and housing offered here largely reflects national data and trends, much of the information contained within the following pages was garnered from staff and clients of Hope House, a social service agency located on the northern border of Kentucky (the names of the agency and its staff members have been changed). The questionable distinction of being among the ten states with the worst child poverty rate belongs to Kentucky; 25 percent of children in Kentucky live in poverty. Related and equally unpalatable is the fact that Kentucky ranked forty-second in state expenditures per child in 1990. These compelling statistics call for an analysis of their impact on the daily lives of children who bear the consequences of their parents' poverty.

This book is a critique of a system that purports to serve yet sometimes impedes the welfare of those who need the basic elements for survival. It is a treatise on poverty and on the lack of affordable housing. Using facts and figures gathered from numerous sources, I analyze the structural factors of poverty as well as the social psychological costs of being poor and lacking a home. In addition to findings from prior research, interviews with staff members and clients of Hope House and my own experience, both as a researcher and as one who has been without a home, are presented. In this work I sound another wake-up call—as many have done before me—about the consequences, for family members, of being without a home. I examine the impact of living on the edge of absolute deprivation for individuals, familial relationships, and children's overall development.

Finally, this book is written by one who has beaten the odds. I have known the fear and anxiety of being without a home, twice as a child and once as a young adult. I know too well that the fear of losing one's home never dissipates. In these pages you will not find a call for people to pull themselves up by their bootstraps. It is a call for *verstehen*, an understanding that for most of those who are poor, either the boots or the straps are missing.

Acknowledgments

This book has been made possible through the cooperation of the executive director of Hope House, Jocelyn Carrington, her dedicated staff, and the women and children who have lived and continue to live through desperate times. I wish to thank Ms. Carrington for permitting me to tell the story of "every" woman and child in this society who suffers the brutal effects of being poor, not only those who walk through the doors of Hope House.

My heartfelt appreciation goes to the women and children who have been assisted by Hope House and who were willing to share their stories with me candidly, thoughtfully, and poignantly.

I am grateful to my colleague, J. Robert Lilly, for his comments and advice during the early stages of this project.

Finally, many thanks to Aunt Clorinda for sheltering me when my family had no place to live. And a very loving thank you to Eiler, Elena, Megan, and Gigi, whose steadfast support has sustained me through all my ventures.

Introduction

If home is where the heart is, are those who are without a home tonight heartless? Are those women who lack a home or receive Aid for Families with Dependent Children the "new prostitutes," as Stephanie Golden suggested?[1] Why do so many of these women not have male partners? Are they bad, irresponsible, or neglectful lovers, spouses, or parents? What did they do to deserve such a fate? Are they lacking family values? Are their mates irresponsible bums?

And what about the children? How does a mother respond to a child who asks if she should call the shelter in which they are huddled, "home"? What does a shelter worker say to a child when she asks "Which shelter do *you* stay in?" How do we explain society's profamily ideology to children who are living in shelters? What words do we use to convince children living in poverty that their society reveres children and the family above all else? How do we reconcile this land of opportunity with a nation in which 5 million children go hungry every day? How can we defend the fact that children are the poorest group of citizens in this country—so poor that 44 percent of poor children live in families whose income is less than half the official poverty level? Can we, as a society, live with the fact that today the United States contains more poor children than in any year since 1965?

Because this nation's value system and ideology are based on individualism and self-made success, we often express sympathy for children who are in poverty or lack a home, but our attention is quickly diverted to their caretakers' perceived indolence. After all, in America we firmly believe that diligence pays off in the form of money, status, power, or all three. Those who are struggling for upward social mobility are reassured by an ideology of individualism which suggests that failure resides in the person, not in the social system. It tells us that we can achieve success if we work hard. Rather than hearing the facts about poverty and about those who are living below the official poverty line, many people would rather believe the myths about lazy women having child after child, driving Cadillacs to pick up their welfare checks, and misusing our hard-earned tax dollars in the process. In reality, fewer than half of the eligible families receive Aid to Families with Dependent Children and the poorest are least likely to take advantage of this federally funded program. The system is not abused—rather, not enough of those who need the system use it.

In this work I urge the reader to discard preconceived notions about the "poor" and to journey with me on the lonely descent to shelter—the incomplete solution for those without homes. I ask the reader to consider the notion of prevention-intervention to stem the tide of families without homes; I also address the efforts of Hope House, a service provider in northern Kentucky that seeks to reverse destabilizing circumstances in client families' lives before they lose their homes.

Bridging the disciplines of sociology and social work, I construct a sociological framework in which I review many of the social conditions that explain the growth in numbers of those in poverty. The reader is offered a social psychological perspective of the impact which living on the precipice of absolute poverty has on women, children, and men. In weaving together the conceptual and the practical, I hope to dispel many of the negative myths about the poor and those without homes.

This book presents the experiences of those who are living in poverty or without homes—especially women and children. The reader will understand more clearly how family stability of those subsisting in poverty is impaired amid the shifting economic and political environment. Much of the discussion centers on temporary shelters, the current (albeit unsatisfactory) solution for a lack of affordable housing. Using a sociological perspective, I describe the cumulative disintegrating effect which poverty, lack of housing, and residence in a shelter has on family relationships

Based on unstructured, open-ended interviews with staff members of Hope House, clients, and client children, this work recounts the stories of these women and children in composite and collage form. Observations gathered from five consciousness-raising sessions with clients and staff of Hope House contribute to the analysis of the many complex issues raised here. Their differing viewpoints are meant to provide an overall perspective of what it is like to be without a home and to live in poverty.

Divided into three parts, this work is ultimately concerned with the consequences of poverty for women and children. However, factors that affect housing availability and family economic solvency must be considered as well. The first section sets the stage by introducing the reader to the changing population and the changes in community conditions for those without homes. Chapter 1 describes the array of factors that decrease available housing for those hovering at the bottom of the income scale. Major issues facing those without housing as well as the systemic conditions affecting people's ability to remain in their homes are summarized. Research findings are offered about those with whom we are more likely to have information—the so-called "traditional" groups without homes—men, alcoholics, and the deinstitutionalized. The reader is then introduced to the relatively new groups living in shelters including growing numbers of families. Finally, the changing skyline of cities wrought by urban renewal since World War II and its impact on affordable housing are examined.

Chapter 2 reflects an effort to dispel negative images about those living in poverty. Prevailing myths about those who live in economic desperation as well as the day-to-day realities of their situations are examined. Also considered is the relationship between the growing inability of men and women to support their families and the loss of housing.

In part II, the focus shifts to a social-psychological examination of the descent to poverty and shelter for mothers and their children. Taking the perspective of twentieth-century sociological giant Erving Goffman, the focus is on mothers in chapter 3. The devastation to a mother's self-concept that accompanies being without a home is analyzed as well as the emotional "paralysis" and depression that ensue because of her inability to provide her children with their basic needs.

In chapter 4, attention is drawn specifically to the plight of children living in shelters and the resulting trauma that affects their future development. Questions are raised about the validity of holding up middle-class standards to judge families who are suffering the effects of poverty. Could most families withstand the exposure and public scrutiny which those subsisting in poverty undergo repeatedly?

In part III, the focus shifts from the emotional and economic despair of those in poverty to a quest for solutions to the ills of poverty at the societal and individual level. Chapter 5 addresses the declining commitment of federal and state revenues for assisting the poor and examines what that means for service providers. Collaborative community projects, the new paradigm for assisting those in need are examined. In the face of diminishing federal dollars, increased efficiency and decreased redundancy has become the mantra for providers. The federal and local directive for coalition building versus competition is examined. The utility and feasibility of resurrecting consciousness-raising as a strategy for altering the collective self-concept of those who exist at subsistence level is considered in chapter 6. Chapter 7 focuses on policy recommendations and solutions to reverse the increased poverty levels and housing shortages.

Finally, in the epilogue, I entreat the reader to employ C. Wright Mills's sociological imagination to connect the private troubles of those in poverty with the systemic problems from which they spring. The treatise concludes with a plea to develop solutions that provide boot straps for those living in poverty, not simply blame the victim.

Part I

DESCENT TO SHELTER: SYSTEMIC FACTORS LEADING TO SHELTER

Chapter 1

How a Diverse Population Grew While Housing Decreased

THOSE WITHOUT HOMES: A CHANGING POPULATION

Before the 1980s, there was little public concern or research about those living without homes. "Skid row" alcoholics and hoboes received most of the attention on this subject. Perceived as a mostly male population, this group had been both romanticized and stigmatized in the popular press, films, and novels. News stories about men hopping trains and setting up camps along railroad tracks and news photos about the king of the hoboes legitimized life without a home as willful and volunteer. As long as those without homes were perceived as primarily men—a population that is expected to provide for itself, to be self-sufficient—little collective concern for their well-being was expressed, and no systemic solutions were sought. Instead, the many places they called home were bulldozed, replaced by office towers, hotels, and upscale retail establishments.

The new Gucci- and Armani-attired transients who now converge upon redefined urban spaces deviate from the thrift shop–appareled indigenous transients who formerly called the areas home. No public outcry had to be stifled when the changing of the guard occurred. Attitudes about the male population without homes were and continue to be cavalier. In fact, in a land fomenting cultural admiration for images like the Marlboro man, for most there is something unnerving and unnatural about a man who cannot be a good provider. In the next few pages, an overview of the literature is presented to acquaint the reader with the old and the new populations of individuals who are surviving without benefit of permanent housing, without a room of their own.

THE OLD POPULATION

Alcoholics without Housing

Although some estimates indicate that about 33 percent of those without homes are alcoholics,[1] circumspection is advised in interpreting the statistics. In many cases, alcohol-imbibing habits are not detected easily unless the individual appears visibly inebriated during most of his or her waking hours, or seeks professional help for the condition. Consequently, it is difficult to know the proportion of alcoholics who are still in their homes, who are closet alcoholics, who have not admitted that they have a problem, or who have yet to "cry uncle" concerning their alcohol abuse.

In other words, because alcoholism comes in many varieties, many forms, a comparison cannot readily be made between the alcoholic population with homes and that without homes. Alcoholism could occur at the same rate for both groups but have a greater detection rate for one. It is important to understand that alcoholism is one factor that explains the loss of housing, but it is not the only explanation.

Therefore, any general statements or causal assertions about the relationship between alcoholism and the loss of housing must be made cautiously. For example, one study found that more than one-quarter of those without homes spent time in a detoxification program before losing their homes,[2] but it is not clear under what conditions people lost their homes or entered the program. The difference between those who lose their homes and those who do not can be the enabling behavior of a significant other or an employer who is in denial. Keep in mind that most persons working in low-skilled jobs would not be provided with medical insurance to pay for alcohol-abuse treatment nor receive discretionary time off from work for detoxification. Indeed, it is highly probable that low-income, low-skilled workers would be either fired or suspended without compensation, which could lead in many instances to loss of home.

The point is that there may be as many alcoholics who live in their homes as there are alcoholics without homes. We cannot know with certainty. And we cannot assume causality; that is, that alcoholism causes the loss of one's home. It is more likely that what the research can tell us is that there is a relationship between the variables. To state that those without homes are alcoholics implies that housing was lost because of individual deficiencies and character flaws. Further, if the group is perceived to be made up of alcoholic men—a population for which self-sufficiency is a societal expectation—their plight is more likely viewed as deserved.

Those Convicted of Crimes

Another group likely to be without a permanent residence and unlikely to receive much empathy are the formerly incarcerated. This group, mostly men, is estimated to make up more than 50 percent of adults without homes.[3] Because the chance of obtaining employment decreases dramatically after one is convicted of a crime, it is surprising that the proportion of former convicts without homes is not higher. Rather than place blame, consider their plight. Theirs is a catch-22 situation: If they reveal their criminal record to a potential employer, they are unlikely to be hired. On the other hand, if they deny that they have a record and the employer makes a background check, they are likely not to be hired, or, if they have obtained the job, they are likely to be fired. When an individual's earning capability is severely constrained or completely destroyed, that person's survival is dubious. Thus it is not surprising that so many of those who have been incarcerated are without homes.

Some reading this might think that a person who has been convicted of a crime deserves whatever occurs as a result of his or her actions. However, our legal system is not predicated on the notion that the punishment go beyond that which satisfies the decision of the judge or jury.

In general, our justice system dictates that deviant behavior be penalized by a variety of methods, including incarceration, probation, fines, suspended sentences, community service, and other sanctions considered appropriate. Under this system, once offenders have paid fully for their debt to society, they can anticipate a resumption of an independent life. Implicit in that expectation is the ability to support oneself economically. Typically, however, those who commit crimes serve two sentences, one in jail and a second when they attempt to begin life anew after incarceration.

Having one's criminal record discovered, however, invites a "spoiled identity."[4] Goffman's treatise about disgrace and the societal categorization of individuals who violate accepted norms is an apt point of reference for the formerly incarcerated. Goffman maintains that one who is stigmatized in society is viewed as less than human:

On this assumption we exercise varieties of discrimination, through which we effectively, if often unthinkingly, reduce his life chances. We construct a stigma-theory, an ideology to explain his inferiority and account for the danger he represents, sometimes rationalizing an animosity based on other differences.[5]

Further, according to Goffman's thinking, if the stigmatized individual reacts defensively to our discriminatory behavior, his response is used by us as justification for our subsequent treatment of him. Therefore, if the "criminalized" individual becomes defensive or hostile because of others' discriminatory behavior toward him or her, this reinforces the discriminators' feelings of righteousness about the treatment they direct at the stigmatized individual.

Those Treated for Mental Health Problems

Another group that has suffered Goffmananian stigmatization includes those who have been hospitalized for mental disorders or who have been treated for a mental health problem. There are some estimates that at least one-third of those adults who are without homes have been hospitalized because of mental illness.[6]

Though the relationship between a diagnosis of mental illness and being without a home is not explicitly examined as causal; that is, that mental illness causes individuals to suffer the loss of their home, a causal relationship is frequently implied. While the sequence of events often occurs in that order, let us examine the issue from another perspective. Imagine for a moment that you have no idea where you will sleep tonight, tomorrow night, or the next, or any night thereafter. Try to visualize some of the issues surrounding being without a home. Think about the issue of physical safety. Sleeping on the street makes one more vulnerable to victimization—assault, robbery, rape, even murder. Existing daily under those circumstances, how do you think you would behave toward strangers?

How well do you think you would sleep night after night worrying about being victimized? How well do you function after one night of sleeplessness? How would you function after a week of sleeplessness? After a month of sleeplessness?

Could you sleep in the rain? How about the cold? How well do you sleep in your bed when you feel cold and a blanket is within your reach? Imagine sleeping on a piece of cardboard on the ground with only a jacket or newspaper over you. Think of how you shiver walking from a comfortably warm building to an ice-covered car on a blustery winter day. Imagine the bone-chilling cold you would experience if you were forced to leave a public library, a soup kitchen, or the bus station, and there is no car waiting for you. What do you think the constant assault of cold weather would do to you when you are already fatigued by sleepless nights?

Where would you bathe, shower, shampoo your hair, brush your teeth? How many changes of clothing do you think you would have? How kempt would you appear? Would you have body odor? What would your daily caloric intake be? Do you think you would take in the federal government's recommended amount of daily vitamins and nutrients? Would you see your dentist two times a year? Would you get a yearly medical check-up?

How would the cold and fatigue affect your mood? Would you be pleasant? Would you be trusting? Would others want to interact with you? Would you be interested in engaging in small talk? Do you think you would begin to appear antisocial to strangers? Do you think being without housing could influence behaviors that might be viewed as symptomatic of mental illness?

Are there people who are without housing because of mental illness? Yes, no doubt about it. But many who are without housing develop clinical depression because of their plight—the uncertainty and unpredictability and their chaotic, terror-ridden existence can bring about a sense of powerlessness, depersonalization, and demoralization. Those without homes are estimated to have a depression rate three to five times higher than the population in general.[7] Again, as with alcoholism, no simplistic assignment of causality can be made.

THE NEWER POPULATION

The Impact of Deinstitutionalization

The so-called deinstitutionalization movement that began in the mid-1950s and escalated in the two decades following has been cited as the most significant factor in the steady rise in the number of individuals with mental health problems living on the street and/or in shelters.[8] As a movement, deinstutionalization was intended to restore the civil rights of those diagnosed as mentally ill and to limit the number of involuntary hospitalizations. By the same token, hundreds of thousands of people were placed back in their communities without sufficient support services to counter the fear, ambivalence, and stigmatization many endured. Some have argued that the problem has been compounded by demographic factors. For example, the bulging baby-boom cohort has contributed significantly to the population of those diagnosed as mentally ill.[9]

Let us ponder for a moment why institutionalization can hinder an individual's standing in the community. First, as social psychologist Erving Goffman would suggest, an institutionalized person is expected to take on the role of a sick, dependent individual. Some people are more likely to acquiesce and submit completely to their confinement and the dependent role; however, doing so makes the transition to an independent life outside the institution less feasible. Because hospitals are total institutions, hospital staff have preconceived expectations about the normative behavior of patients. Hospital staff expect patients to be for the most part compliant, obedient, and unquestioning of hospital authority. Those patients who enact appropriate behavior are rewarded, and those who do not are negatively sanctioned.[10] The book and subsequent film *One Flew Over the Cuckoo's Nest* effectively illustrates that point. Undoubtedly, to assist with the transition from total institution to total freedom, more transitional housing is needed to allow individuals without support systems to gradually reintegrate into the community.

Second, because of our society's largely negative attitude toward mental illness, postinstitutional adjustment may be extremely difficult, even under the best circumstances. Once people have been diagnosed or labeled, their behavior is viewed constantly through a diagnostic lens. Any emotion exhibited—anger, fear, joy—becomes suspect and subject to dissection. The slightest deviance from the norm is tolerated less well in a diagnosed person than in one without a diagnosis. Again, Goffman's notion of stigmatization is useful here.

Without Community Support: Housing Remains an Issue

Until our society acquires a greater understanding and acceptance of mental illness, individuals with a history of mental illness will fare little better after institutionalization than the formerly incarcerated population. Evidence shows that the more funding is available in a city to support residential centers for those with chronic mental difficulties, the less likely housing will be problematic for deinstitutionalized individuals.[11]

Having a community-based support system in place in addition to housing is a must for individuals who have been released from hospitalization. The support system ideally should include a means to continue medication and therapeutic treatment, emotional support for the individual, and, when possible, a job in the community. The discussion thus far has focused on the traditional groups without homes whose plight has failed to dent our social conscience. Unfortunately, these groups have earned the mantle of the "deservedly wretched" among us. The reader's attention is now turned to emerging groups living without housing who have stirred national interest.

THE NEWEST POPULATION

Women: The New People on the Street

Until recently, women were absent from any discussion about those needing a home. In fact women without homes were largely invisible. In the past, patriarchal attitudes have been manifested in an assumption that women are cared for by fathers, husbands, brothers, or uncles, and thus should not be in need of housing. Even today, society assumes that women are deeply embedded in the family and the domestic sphere. As a result, women without homes generally have not been perceived as street people in the same way as men. The term *bag lady*, a relatively new pejorative expression, connotes mental instability rather than degenerate status (as does *skid row bum*). Thus, from a patriarchal perspective, it has been assumed that women were not at risk of losing their homes unless they had done something to "deserve being kicked out," such as committing adultery or being an unfit mother. Because women have been overlooked among those on the street, we have had little solid information concerning the extent to which they have exchanged and continue to exchange housekeeping, sex, or both for shelter for themselves and their children.

More New People on the Street: Families

Today, two-parent families are surfacing increasingly among those in need of shelter.[12] I use the term *surfacing* because, as one who was without a home three times during the 1950s, I believe that my family's plight was not unique. It simply went undetected in a society that denies its problems until they reach colossal proportions.

Because our society has ignored or denied the existence of a housing crisis for decades, the stock of low-income housing has dwindled and increasing numbers of people are without homes. One report purports that 50,000 to 500,000 children belong to this group.[13] Today it is estimated that families constitute about 35 percent of those without homes. In some areas the proportion is much higher; in Massachusetts, for example, families make up about 75 percent of the homeless.[14] Meanwhile, as individuals live in chaos, the housing issue is discussed and debated by government agencies, state and local legislatures, service providers, and the media. And funds that could be targeted toward alleviating their desperation continue to disappear.

The bottom line is that increasingly those without homes are a varied population. Included are those suffering from alcoholism (assumed to be primarily men), the formerly incarcerated (also assumed to be mostly men), those who have been institutionalized at some time (women and men), females (both single women and female heads of household), husbands, wives, and their children. Because this is a heterogenous group, monolithic solutions will not do. Permanent housing needs of individuals differ from the needs of families. These factors complicate the formulation and implementation of solutions.

Young Families and Poverty

What other factors contribute to the likelihood of being without a home? More and more, being young and undereducated plays a role.

In fact, between the early 1970s and 1986, the largest increase in poverty occurred among young families. The younger the family, the greater the likelihood of poverty.[15] This last point means that today's young people are less and less likely to surpass their parents' standard of living. As evidence of this discouraging assessment, the average age of those who are without homes has declined from the forties to the midthirties.[16] Thus it appears that at least some of the baby boomers, a group whose affluence is consistently overstated, have passed their poverty, not their wealth, to the next generation.

Education and Poverty

Because education is considered the great equalizer and a major factor in upward social mobility, it is important in predicting economic solvency. Kathleen Mullan Harris found that multiple factors affect economic well-being, including education, number of children, and marital status.[17] We know that half of those families whose breadwinner lacks a high school diploma are in poverty. Unfortunately, despite such grim statistics, individuals continue to drop out of high school; at least 25 percent do not finish. In heavily populated cities, the dropout rate can be as high as 60 percent.

WHERE HAS ALL THE AFFORDABLE HOUSING GONE?

Urban Renewal: For Whom?

Most of the national debate about people without adequate, affordable housing has focused on their numbers and their characteristics. Although it is important to know who is without a home and whether the population has changed over time, we also must know how strongly extrafamilial factors have affected families' ability to obtain safe, affordable housing. Clearly, the supply of affordable housing determines who has a home and who does not.

Since the 1960s, with the initiation of the war on poverty and then-President Lyndon Johnson's Great Society, urban renewal has redefined many of our nation's metropolitan skylines. Much to the despair of those living in central cities, renewal brought new inhabitants as well as new structures. Over time, low-cost living units rented by impoverished neighborhood populations have been replaced with high-rise office towers occupied only about one-third of the day by commuting suburbanites. High-priced hotel rooms inhabited by transient, out-of-town individuals have replaced the single-room-occupancy hotels (SROs) that were home to impoverished women and men. It is estimated that more than a million living units have been lost to demolition in cities across the country. Perhaps the hardest hit have been the SROs; cities such as Los Angeles, Boston, and Seattle lost most of their rooming houses in their urban renewal blitz. In the process, neighborhoods were destroyed or molded into unrecognizable forms.[18]

In the northern tip of Kentucky, no antidemolition ordinance exists to deflect the wrecking ball. Low-income housing continues to be threatened by commercial development, gentrification, and road projects. If residential devastation occurred because of war or natural disaster, public sympathy and financial assistance would be forthcoming. Instead, the dislocated must fight for whatever little public and private assistance they can obtain to begin life anew. To compound the distress caused by urban renewal, federal support for low-income housing was cut by more than two-thirds during the early 1980s.[19] With the current Congress, more cuts are forthcoming.

The shortfall of housing units for low-income households is estimated at about 5 million. Doug Timmer, Stanley Eitzen, and Kathryn Talley maintain that if the current low-income housing stock continues to disappear, 19 million people will be left without homes. They report that between 1981 and 1988 federal funding for subsidized housing diminished by 80 percent.[20] In Kentucky a 1990 report by the Northern Kentucky Housing and Homeless Coalition maintained that 2,000 affordable housing units needed to be constructed by the year 2000. To date, however, construction has not reached 10 percent of the recommended number. Compounding the lag in new construction is the fact that at least 35 percent of the existing housing stock in northern Kentucky is substandard, making the housing situation even more tenuous for those in poverty. The bottom line is that the housing market is not constructing affordable housing for low-income households.[21]

Decreases in federal funds for construction of public housing continue to exacerbate the problem. Low-income housing is supported by one federal dollar for every three dollars received by middle- and upper-income homeowners through mortgage interest deductions and tax subsidies. Even more telling, those with annual incomes above $100,000 receive more than 33 percent of these subsidies. Waiting periods for low-cost rental housing are longer now than in the past.[22] Yet despite these inequities, at this writing, the mood in the Congress and in the White House favors dismantling federal assistance for those living in poverty.

Boarding Houses: Once Popular Home Away from Home

Boarding houses and rooms for rent in private homes, both common fixtures in the early American landscape, began to disappear from cities even before the great urban renewal was initiated. As a result, large numbers of individuals were left without homes. Typically this form of housing provided a relatively inexpensive, safe home environment for those migrating from rural areas to urban centers and for immigrants from other countries. Nineteenth- and early twentieth-century census data give evidence of their acceptance as forms of housing. Boarding houses and rental rooms not only provided affordable housing for hundreds of thousands of people, but also enabled families to earn income without forcing the wife and/or mother to leave hearth and children.[23]

Even as late as the turn of the century, rooms in private homes were considered a haven above reproach for young migrant women. During that period, unattached, young women moving to urban areas were regarded as vulnerable to the corruption lurking in the city. And lone females without benefit of family sponsorship were viewed with suspicion, even deviant. Women without family or other ties were considered less desirable tenants than lone males. To preserve their reputation and their character, most of the single women who ventured to the city lived with nonrelated families. It is estimated that more than half of young migrant women lived with families in private residences and about 29 percent of unattached women in large urban centers lived in boarding houses in the late nineteenth century.[24]

Interestingly, while social reformers believed that quality housing was necessary in order for native-born young migrant women to preserve both their physical health and their moral integrity, no public outcry was heard for the safety of poor immigrant women or African-American women. In fact, many homes refused to house these groups. It is instructive that today, more than a century later, a similar population is heavily represented in temporary housing facilities because of a lack of permanent homes. And today, as in the past, the voices raised to protest these conditions are less than deafening.

Single-Room-Occupancy Hotels

Living arrangements that were commonplace in the nineteenth century began to change drastically after World War II and continued to change well into the 1980s. San Francisco's South of Market neighborhood, for example, lost homes for thousands of residents as well as hundreds of small businesses. Hotels and office complexes were constructed in their place. South of Market had been home to many single elderly men who were retired or disabled, but the press and local officials had referred to these residents as "bums, drifters, and transients."[25] Negative terms operate to depersonalize members of a group and give others permission to treat the members as less than human.

This scenario was repeated again and again in the post–World War II urban renewal frenzy. For the most part, the boarding houses and SROs left standing in the wake of urban renewal eventually succumbed to local zoning laws and regulations that limited the location of multiple-family dwellings. While the changes due to urban renewal and zoning explain a major part of the increase in the numbers of people who lack homes, other factors must be considered as well.

Demographic Causes

Demographic characteristics that could be expected to lessen the housing crisis in central cities—outmigration and decline in fertility—have not done so. Two opposing forces appear to be operating in central cities. For those at the lower end of the income scale, the remaining affordable housing stock, having survived urban renewal thus far, continues to decay. At the upper end, gentrification in central cities has increased the number (albeit there is a smaller proportion) of nonpoor residents. Through rehabbing, property values are pushed upward. As a result, upper-income newcomers are making the area less accessible to poor persons. It is instructive that while upscale housing has increased, the average number of persons living in each household has decreased from 2.76 in 1980 to 2.63 in 1990.[26] In cities, then, income bifurcation has occurred, with a large proportion of the population living in poverty and a smaller but increasing proportion of higher-income gentrifiers infiltrating inner cities. In summarizing, low-income housing stock continues to disappear in the cities, and a proportion that is left is being rehabbed for upper-income folks, thus exacerbating housing problems for the poor.

Cost: Another Prohibitive Housing Factor

It has been argued that many people in this country, if not most, are two paychecks away from being without a home. Frightening as that statement is, it is a realistic assessment. Many workers have experienced a decline in full-time work and simultaneously the spiraling cost of housing. More to the point, the median monthly rent increased by 192 percent during the 1970s and early 1980s, while monthly earnings increased by only half that figure.[27] The experience of residents in northern Kentucky reflects national averages: rent for a two-bedroom apartment averaged between $424 and $525 per month in the late eighties. In order to afford a market-rate, two-bedroom apartment, an individual must work full-time at $9.00 an hour. Increasing numbers of individuals working part-time at minimum wage cannot qualify for a two-bedroom apartment. Many could not qualify for a one-bedroom apartment, which requires full-time employment at about $7.50 an hour.

Researchers Marta Elliott and Lauren J. Krivo found that individuals are at greater risk of being without a home in areas with a higher proportion of minimally skilled jobs.[28] Using C. Wright Mills's sociological imagination, lower wages compounded with higher costs of housing do not indicate individual inadequacy. Rather, they reflect systemic problems over which individuals have no control.[29] Individual economic solvency is becoming increasingly difficult for more and more families in an economically hostile environment. Unfortunately, rather than attacking systemic economic issues, which are heightened by increasing competition over scarce resources, the national debate focuses on poor individuals lacking personal responsibility.

Structural and institutional factors affecting housing availability are intertwined with housing costs. At the individual level, people cope with economic uncertainty in the best way they can. For example, persons with relatively high incomes often live in lower-rent apartments.[30] Others stay in apartments because their income or credit history does not qualify them for a home loan. About 57 percent of those who rent cannot get a 30-year loan for a house that is median priced.[31] Because the cost of housing has increased dramatically, from 15 percent of earnings in the 1950s to 40 percent today, it makes economic sense, for example, to maximize income targeted for basic needs. Yet the savings realized by those who could afford more costly housing decreases the affordable housing stock available to the poorest segment of the population. About 10 million people were seeking low-income housing by the 1980s.[32]

Unfortunately, economic conditions that threaten to force people over the edge of despair are a reality for a growing number of American citizens, especially children. In the next chapter, some of the myths and realities for families in poverty are examined.

Chapter 2

Family Values and Other Myths and Realities about Families

The focus of this work is the plight of women and their children who are without permanent housing. However, in order to have a sense of *verstehen* about their lives, the reader needs to have an appreciation for the events that preceded the descent to shelter for so many families. Many factors that have an impact on the lives of women and children have more to do with the economic circumstances of the husbands and fathers of these desperate families and will be examined in this chapter. But before turning our attention to the material conditions of families on the brink of disaster, some of the political rhetoric and persistent societal myths surrounding families who are poor will be considered.

FAMILY VALUES

Are family values a thing of the past? Listening to today's politicians about the declining significance people place on family life, one would think so. However, at all times and in all societies, family values and the status of family morality have been debated and the subject of political discourse. Indeed, United States history is replete with such discussions. It is within the last century that the prevailing ideology dictated a woman's proper place should be embedded in a family system. Women daring enough to flaunt a lifestyle deviating from that model were suspect. At least one illustration of the ideology of women as family centered is George Ellington's observations of unattached women in New York during that era.[1] According to Ellington, lone women were perceived as immoral and suspect. Far from the exception, Ellington's observations were shared by his contemporaries. Social reformer types of his time expressed concern about women who, for whatever reason, left hearth and home to join the paid labor force. Much hand wringing was done about the degrading effects of the workplace on women's morality. Fearing that women would be corrupted by the vulgar behavior of their male co-workers, making them unfit for motherhood, most people of the late nineteenth century believed woman's place was in the house.[2]

Although we have not veered too far from the ideology that asserts a woman's place is in the home where her morality can be protected, most women cannot afford to stay in the home. What has developed, then, is a bifurcated view of women's role. Conservatives lament what they perceive as the demise of the family and blame mom's labor-force participation. On the other hand, women in poverty get another kind of message—to get up and go to work. Late twentieth-century debate has directed moralistic chastisement on families of lower socioeconomic status and fathers who do not provide for their families.

Recently, debate about family values erupted among national politicians, more precisely, Republican House Speaker Newt Gingrich and President Clinton. They engaged in a media-oriented exchange concerning the issue of "welfare reform." Amid diatribes about cutting aid to families living in poverty and decreased spending on school lunch programs for children, oddly, Clinton and Gingrich seemed in agreement in their perception that the nation's family values were being compromised by multiple factors, including absent fathers, welfare, and the media, especially television.

The Clinton-Gingrich political haggling followed on the heels of the national media family- values frenzy surrounding the 1992 presidential campaign. Then -Vice President Dan Quayle attacked a television series in which the fictional character Murphy Brown had a child outside of marriage. His criticism drew mixed responses. Conservatives extolled what they perceived as Quayle's profamily stance, while liberals condemned his remarks as an indictment against single, female heads of household. Soon researchers and scholars joined the fray, with the likes of David Popenoe and Judith Stacey debating the status of the family as an institution.[3] Too, almost a century after Ellington, many of the expectations for women have not diverged from the earlier paradigm. Like Ellington before her, Golden has observed that women who are alone—without a man and/or without a home—are perceived as violating a sex-role norm and thus are judged as deserving their plight.[4] Accused of becoming too individualistic because of working outside of the home, women are perceived by some as having lost their collective spirit—a quality important for nurturing a family.[5] It is an ongoing dilemma for women, especially poor women. If they do not work to support their children, women are viewed as lazy and irresponsible. If, on the other hand, they join the paid labor force (as working-class and middle-class women have), women are labeled as uncommitted to family values. In the midst of the debate about whether a wife and mother should work, one study suggests that women who work and earn above the minimum wage may have chosen a surer way out of poverty than marriage.[6] Finding a partner who can be the sole support of a family is becoming more difficult as the good-provider role becomes more elusive for men as discussed later in the chapter. For now, the reader's attention is turned to the mythological treatment of poverty.

MYTHS ABOUT THE POOR PERSIST

Myths that develop about those who are living in poverty are related to what Berger and Luckmann refer to as a second ideology. According to this author team, dual ideologies emerge in society: one that safeguards the elite, and another that blames the problems of the have-nots on their supposed immorality or character flaws.[7] Contemporary debate about the poor is filled with references to morality and deficiencies of the individual. A few myths are addressed here.

Myth: Women Have Children to Obtain More Welfare Assistance

Perhaps the most widespread myth of the late twentieth century is that women receiving Aid to Families with Dependent Children produce many children to collect large government checks. Although statistics do not support such a characterization of women who are poor, the myth persists. In fact, the number of children born to women who receive AFDC reflects national trends. Among families below the poverty line who receive assistance, 42 percent have only one child; another 30 percent have two children. If anything, these figures show that those who are poor fall sway to the same cultural imperatives that women in other social classes do. All members of a society, rich or poor, internalize, to a great extent, the values of their culture. And most tend not to deviate widely from normative behavior, that is, behavior deemed acceptable by their society's standards. The decision to have a child, then, is an economic decision intertwined with societal values. The total fertility rate in the United States illustrates that point quite well. The rate has hovered around 1.9 in this country for almost a decade, indicating that having several children is no longer considered economically and emotionally desirable by most people.

Following up on that point is a recent Children's Defense Fund report reaching the same conclusion;[8] that is, that those who are economically deprived follow societal dictums and act in ways similar to other social classes. The report indicates that in 1989 women receiving Aid to Families with Dependent Children had an average of 1.9 children. Further, the report stated that a woman is increasingly less likely to have more children the longer she receives governmental assistance. A second child adds about $2.27

per day to a mother's assistance check. Under these circumstances, few women see having additional children as a benefit.

Recent immigrant groups whose culture of origin supports or advocates larger families tend to have more children than those who are native born. But typically second- and third-generation immigrants have fewer children than the first generation because of the effect of being socialized in their adopted culture and subjected to the same messages, direct and indirect, that others are. From primary caretakers, teachers, peers, co-workers, and the media come reinforcing messages concerning the economic and psychological costs of raising children today. The message is clear: having fewer children is desirable and more economically feasible.

Myth: The Poor Get Rich on Welfare

Another myth related to the "many children" myth is that families receiving government assistance are getting rich. The reality is that even with monthly income assistance and food stamp allotments, families are unable to pay for their minimal needs. In fact, the average family receiving AFDC in 1992 collected a monthly check totaling $136 per person, compared with $166 in 1970 (in Kentucky, the total amount for a mother and two children was $228). And the average monthly food stamp amount in 1992 was $66 per person (in Kentucky, a mother and two children receive $292 a month in food stamps). Table 2.1 aptly illustrates the percentage decrease in the dollar amount of AFDC transfer payments since 1970 for selected states.

If AFDC is computed on a yearly basis, the dismal reality is even more striking—the average benefit for a family of three in 1993 was $4,400 a year, or $6,900 below the official poverty level (in Kentucky, which ranks 44th in the amount of transfer payments allowed, the maximum benefit a family of three can receive is $228 a month, or $2,736 a year, $8,564 below the poverty line). Tragically, government transfer payments nationwide are so meager that rather than the disadvantaged getting rich fewer than 10 percent of young children are rescued from poverty by AFDC. As table 2.2

Table 2.1

States in which AFDC Maximum Monthly Benefit for a Three-Person Family Dropped More than 50 Percent, 1970–1995 (Adjusted for Inflation)

State	Percent
Texas	67.0
Idaho	61.0
Kentucky	60.0
Virginia	59.2
Pennsylvania	58.8
Illinois	57.8
South Dakota	57.7
Tennessee	57.1
Wyoming	56.1
Colorado	51.9
North Carolina	51.3

Source: The State of America's Children Yearbook 1996 (Washington, D.C.: Children's Defense Fund), p. 4.

indicates, children are the least likely of all age groups to leave the ranks of the poor through government assistance. As meager as federal assistance has been, the Senate bill signed by President Clinton ends welfare as we know it and is scheduled to cut federal poverty programs by $56 billion over the next few years.

In spite of efforts by service providers, community advocates, and other groups lobbying Congress for increases in spending to boost federal transfer payments, the myth that poor families get rich from AFDC prevails. Not only does it prevail, but it gains potency at various times, especially during pre-election congressional and presidential debates. The myth persists despite periodic reports that little welfare fraud or misuse is found, even when the most advanced technology is used to investigate possible fraud.

Table 2.2

Percentage of People Lifted Out of Poverty by Government Benefit Payments, by Age, 1990

Age	Percent
<6	9
< 18	12
45-64	39
65 and older	74

Source: The State of America's Children 1992 (Washington, D.C.: Children's Defense Fund), p. 28.

Myth: Those on Welfare Are Lazy

According to still another myth, women who are poor are lazy and do not want to work to support their children. Yet many, if not most, of those receiving assistance have worked at various jobs in the hope of becoming self-sufficient. Many simply cannot find a job. In economically distressed areas such as central cities, the ratio of unemployed far out paces the ratio of available jobs, sometimes as much as 8 to 1.[9] Although most never become cognizant that they belong to quite a large majority of women—66 percent of female workers whose wages are at minimum-wage level—women workers soon understand that becoming economically independent through their wages is nearly impossible. Many may not know whether their income falls below the government's official poverty level (or know what the official poverty level is), but they know that their meager earnings will not obtain the necessities for their families.[10] The Children's Defense Fund reported that a single parent with two children would have to earn $20,000 to "make" it. Unfortunately, the ratio of unemployed searching for available minimum-wage jobs is 6 to 1.[11] Women, especially, learn all too quickly that work does not bring them sufficient economic rewards, and rarely the same monetary rewards as it offers to men.

Women have taken for granted that their wages will not equal men's even when doing the same job; however, a growing cadre of working men are experiencing, for the first time, insecurity about their ability to take care of their families.

FAMILIES FACE HARSH ECONOMIC REALTIES

Families and Declining Self-Sufficiency:
Younger Families Fare Worse

As noted in chapter 1, being young increases a family's economic vulnerability. Between the early 1970s and 1986, the largest increase in poverty occurred among young families. The younger the family, the greater the likelihood of poverty.[12] The point is that today's young people may be less likely to surpass their parents' standard of living.

Table 2.3

Poverty Rates in Young Families, 1973 and 1990 (Families Headed by Someone Younger than 30)

	1973	1990
All	20	40
Married	8	20
High school graduate	13	33

Source: The State of America's Children 1992 (Washington, D.C.: Children's Defense Fund), p. 26.

Table 2.3 illustrates the increase in poverty rates for those under 30. These discouraging statistics explain why the average age of those who are without homes has declined from the forties to the midthirties.[13] This unwelcome information means that at least some of the baby boomers, a group whose affluence is consistently overstated, have passed their poverty, not wealth, to the next generation.

Table 2.3 illustrates the increase in poverty rates since the 1970s that has occurred in young families. It appears that having a high school education is not enough to stave off poverty. Timmer, Eitzen, and Talley report that the median wages of family heads under age 25 decreased 60 percent between the 1970s and the 1980s.[14] Table 2.4 shows the percent change in weekly earnings of men between 1974 and 1994. These findings help explain why young men are waiting longer to get married.

Table 2.4

Change in Median Weekly Earnings of Men Employed Full-Time, by Age, 1974–1994 (Adjusted for Inflation)

Age Group	Percent Change
Under 25	-29.8
25-34	-20.9
35-44	-8.1
45-54	+3.8
55-64	+3.0

Source: U.S. Department of Labor, Bureau of Labor Statistics. Calculations by Center for Labor Market Studies, Northeastern University. In *The State of America's Children Yearbook 1996* (Washington, D.C.: Children's Defense Fund), p. 48.

Because traditionally the decline in economic well-being of families has depended on the employment status of fathers, it is important to examine the situation of men. As the table illustrates, men's employment opportunity structure is rocky to say the least, especially for young men. Their economic security has steadily declined since the sixties. In fact, during the 1960s, only 26 percent of Anglo men age 20 to 34 had insufficient income to support a family. But by the end of the 1980s, this figure had climbed to 34 percent.[15] And in 1994, couples with children had a median income that was at least 2 percent less than what it was in 1974.[16] Indeed, between 1973 and 1983, the poverty rate doubled for young couples with children.[17] No matter how the statistics are presented, economically, families do not fare as well as they did 30 years ago.

Education, considered the great equalizer and a major factor in upward mobility, is an important predictor of economic well-being. At least one study by Greg Duncan and Willard Rodgers found that while two factors that generally push up earnings were occurring—increasing levels of education and decreasing number of children—their effect was offset by diminished relative wages, decreasing age of parents, and an increase in one-parent families.[18] Lending support to Duncan and Rodgers's work is the telling statistic that half of those families whose breadwinner lacks a high school diploma are living in poverty. Of those who earn minimum wage, about 39 percent lack a high school diploma.[19] Unfortunately, there is little information to indicate that high school graduates fare little better than those who drop out.

Consider the economic situation of all rank-and-file workers (without controlling for age and education) for the last two decades. Their average weekly earnings (adjusted for inflation) declined from $315 to $258 between 1973 and 1995. Yet during that same time period, output per person increased by 25 percent. This represents the first time in this nation's postwar period that workers' real earnings have failed to match their increased productivity. While workers found themselves in a tightening economic vise between 1979 and 1989, by 1988, the income of corporate chief executives was more than 70 times that of manufacturing workers.[20]

Why Lower Wages?

Although the literature explaining the disproportionate ratio of income of chief executives to wages of workers is scanty, multiple explanations have been generated to rationalize the declining wages and worth of workers. A few will be delineated here.

The reduction in the earnings of workers is frequently explained in terms of the changing structure of the labor market. The structural changes, including the continued shift to service-sector jobs and the decline in manufacturing opportunities, are cited as major reasons for the increase in low-skill, low-paying jobs. Another explanation offered is the transformation of traditionally well-paying manufacturing jobs into lower-paying jobs through mimicking Japanese work organizations.

Lean (mean?) production. Even in the manufacturing industry, relatively higher-waged positions have declined as corporations continue to adopt Japan's lean production methods. Lean production does not necessitate advanced educational qualifications or high skill levels. What lean-production employers find desirable in a worker is manual dexterity, the energy and enthusiasm of a cheerleader, and a willingness to be a team player.[21] In fact, the shift from semi-skilled and skilled, higher-waged employees to less skilled workers who can be paid less is part of what makes lean production so attractive to manufacturers.

While American corporations have demonstrated a proclivity for Japan's style of lean production and management, they have yet to embrace Japan's flattened pay structure. A chief executive officer in Japan, for example, earns 17 times what the average worker does.[22] On the other hand in the United States, where a more hierarchical pay structure operates, the average chief executive receives 85 times what the average factory worker earns. One study found that in 1960 the CEOs earned about 40 times what the average factory worker earns, but by the late eighties it was 93 times.[23] Many top executives earn much more. For example, one airline's top executive receives 1,200 times the income of his flight attendants.[24] While politicians may question the nation's family values, workers might be inclined to question corporate and executive greed.

Men's economic security and good-provider role are increasingly jeopardized in today's market. Yet rather than demanding that corporate pay structures be made more equitable, workers, fearing the loss of their job, adapt and adjust their lives to the sacrifices the workplace demands of them. In essence, they take it on the chin.

Outsourcing, another management strategy. A corollary to lean production that has consequences for the status of workers is the system of contracting out, or outsourcing. This manufacturing tactic means that a large percentage of needed components are produced by a firm other than the initiating firm. The initiating company contracts with as many firms as it needs to in order to complete the manufacturing process. Two leading automakers, Toyota and Chrysler, are examples of companies that use outsourcing. Both contract out about 70 percent of their production. Because the contracting firms use multiple suppliers, smaller firms are under constant threat of losing a contract. Multiple suppliers help drive down the cost for the major manufacturer,[25] but can affect the profit margin of the smaller firm negatively as it attempts to outbid the competition to safeguard its contract. Outsourcing allows a company to have fewer employees for its leaner, "permanent" work force, a strategy that proves to be profitable for a company's shareholders. Rather than a help to workers, outsourcing typically means that people will be employed in a firm that is nonunion, lower paying, and often without benefits.

A PARADIGM SHIFT:
THE DECLINE OF THE GOOD-PROVIDER ROLE

Because the economy continues to be restructured toward the likes of lean production, outsourcing, and service-type jobs, fewer families have the luxury of relying on only one provider for sustenance. As a result, in the last three decades women have been joining the work force in large numbers. Most women who have done so work out of a sense of responsibility for their families, not because (as some observers suggest) they are disregarding their families or relinquishing their domestic roles.[26] In fact the evidence indicates overwhelmingly that women (even those in the paid labor force) continue to do the lion's share of unpaid labor in the home. Rather than shirk responsibility for their family, women work a dual shift—one in the paid labor force and one in the unpaid labor market.[27] While women's financial contribution has kept more families from falling into poverty, most of the increase in family poverty since 1979 has occurred in households in which both spouses are present.[28] Even stranger is the fact that while economic reality for men and women is being altered, woman's role continues to be narrowly defined as that of nurturer and the man's role as that of the good provider. Sadly, despite broad economic changes that severely constrain the ability of men to be good providers, our society continues to expect that men, not women, are to be financially responsible for their children. Men and women whose daily lives attest to the fact that traditional scripts can no longer be played out receive little institutional or social support.

Politicos, including former Republican Vice President Dan Quayle, Democratic President Bill Clinton, and even Islamic leader Louis Farrakhan, have expressed little empathy for the plight of families and the dramatic changes men and women have faced and continue to face. Little has been done to assuage this nation's families, especially husbands and fathers, many of whom are at a disadvantage educationally, economically, and generationally, as the world they know ceases to exist. Instead, fathers who do not provide financially for their children continue to be publicly chastised. Political and spiritual leaders are not alone in their reprisal of fathers. A few social scientists maintain that one measure of the decline of the family is the proportion of fathers who do not support their offspring.[29] The tragic reality, as noted several places in this work, is that an ever-smaller proportion of fathers earn enough to do so.

Rather than haranguing women and men about their supposed lack of family values, we would do better to demonstrate Weber's *verstehen*, empathically acknowledging the plight of families. Those in leadership roles would do well to develop family-friendly policies in the face of an increasing probability that fewer men will be able to carry single-handedly the burden of supporting their family. Women, men, and their governments—state, federal, and local—will have to work together to help families approach a standard of living similar to that of the previous generation. Families, whatever the form, need to have leaders build them up, not denigrate them and obfuscate their attempt to find stability.

The traditional good-provider role has been narrowly defined, so as a man's ability to fulfill this role is eroded, so too are related roles such as husband and father.[30] If fewer men are able to meet the standard of good provider, it is little wonder that men are giving up related roles. We are in the cross hairs of a paradigm shift, of creating a new family ideology—an ideology that addresses the family as an economic partnership involving women, men, and children. At least one study estimated that only one-third of men between ages 25 and 34 are likely to have better jobs than their fathers.[31] Timmer, Eitzen, and Talley report that a survey of the Fortune 500 companies employed almost 4 million fewer workers in 1991 than in 1981.[32] Are our leaders listening?

The Harsh Realities of Providers

Workers feel economically squeezed, but no one is loosening the vise, least of all employers. Instead, today, only a few years from the beginning of a new millennium, employers express concern that unemployment is dangerously low. Managers and corporate heads anguish over fewer workers waiting in the wings for jobs, fearing it could lead to greater demands in the form of wages, benefits, and control. Indeed, when the most recent economic indicators for 1996 were announced, including the lowest unemployment rate in six years, the stock market took a 114-point dive. Investors fear low unemployment might drive up wage demands and inflation.[33] It is instructive that in the face of economic indicators like a low unemployment rate and investors' anxiety, President Clinton and the Congress have paved the way to send millions more workers into the marketplace, workers lacking marketplace skills and without federal assistance for job creation.

Those who are already in the workplace have multiple fears. They have experienced mergers, acquisitions, hostile takeovers, plant closings, downsizing, right-sizing, the demise of unions, a growing proportion of part-time and/or temporary jobs, offshore manufacturing, and lean, mean production. All of these factors have the potential to affect their long-term employment status. As if that were not enough, despite reports indicating that workers' productivity has accelerated, their purchasing power has decreased.[34] It is as though employees are working harder and more efficiently, yet remumeration for their efforts does not reflect their efficiency. While corporate actors would chafe at the suggestion, others maintain that the extent to which productivity increases faster than real wages is a measure of worker exploitation.[35]

Redefining the Unemployment Rate

The uncertain economic circumstances of workers appears not to trouble employers. They are troubled more by low unemployment rates and the dwindling reserve army of job seekers, fearing a demand for higher wages on the part of employees. However, employers need not worry. Because the unemployment rate undercounts those who are not working in several ways, the reserve army is larger than official statistics indicate. First, the unemployment rate does not account for discouraged workers—people who have given up looking for a suitable job. Second, it does not consider those who are underemployed, that is, those who want to work full-time but can find only part-time or temporary work (a growing population, as already noted). Further, the unemployment rate does not include those who cannot find a job that pays enough to support a family (another growing population). Lastly, the rate does not include women who would work if they had affordable child care.

If all of these categories of people were included in the unemployment rate, the figure would approach recession level for Anglo workers and worse for African-Americans. Under the current measure, African-Americans' unemployment rate is more than twice that of Anglos (10 and 4.6 percent respectively),[36] so that it consistently approaches recession level. On any given day then, many

African-American men and their families live with one foot on the brink of economic disaster. And if teens, who consistently have higher unemployment rates than other populations, are considered, African American teens fare worst of all. Their unemployment rate tends to hover at levels indicative of the Great Depression—fluctuating between 20 and 45 percent.

Part-Time Work Will Not Work

All workers (but especially those with families to support) have reason to be concerned when reviewing employment prospects. Service work, which is notoriously low paying, is the fastest-growing sector of the economy and is increasingly part-time. According to Stephanie Coontz, part-time workers increased by 121 percent between 1970 and 1990.[37] Can discouraged or underemployed job seekers be induced into taking the many low-wage, part-time, dead-end, no-benefit jobs that go begging? Women and men who need full-time work, above-minimum wages, and benefits to support their families cannot be good providers in jobs that lack these qualities. It is a conundrum! While employers fear low unemployment rates, for workers, competition is daunting for jobs that would not be considered desirable for a head of household. A recent Children's Defense Fund report (1996) indicates that a study of fast-food restaurants found that only one in thirteen people who applied for available jobs were hired.[38] Further, the study found that of those rejected, 73 percent were without a job a year later. Astonishingly, the list of rejectees included high school graduates and those who had prior work experience.

Part-time Work Leads to Disappearing Benefits

Almost 14 million full-time jobs were created in the decade of the 1980s. However, most required lower skill and offered low wages and few benefits. Many of the mid-range-paying jobs have disappeared. There are more in the higher-paying categories and more at the bottom, but few in the middle.[39] The growth of temporary jobs has been another factor in the demise of lucrative benefit packages for workers. Temporary jobs increased by 250 percent during the 1980s, while employment overall increased by less than 20 percent. The statistics for health insurance coverage illustrate the inequity among workers; only 20 percent of part-time employees are covered, in contrast to 78 percent of full-time workers. However, if new jobs are considered, only 15 percent had health benefits and 38 percent had pensions in 1988, down considerably since 1979.[40] Service and production workers are least likely to receive employment benefits.[41]

When employers offer benefits, employees frequently must refuse them because the cost to them would leave workers with too little income to cover their basic needs. Families then are forced to choose among health care, food, and shelter. At least one family member must work full-time to support a family, but the restructuring of the American economy has denied many men and women the chance to do so.

AFRICAN-AMERICAN MEN AND THE GOOD-PROVIDER ROLE

The Economic Dilemma of African-American Providers

If economic well-being is linked to family formation, African-American men are least likely to be able to take on the male familial role as it is currently prescribed. They are more likely than Anglo men to lose their jobs because of economic restructuring. And younger African-American men suffer most.[42] Thirty years after the civil rights legislation, the economic situation for many African-American men has not significantly improved. Indeed, there is evidence that in fact it may have worsened. For example, in the mid-1960s less than half of African-American men had income insufficient to support a family. By the late 1980s, this figure had risen to 56 percent.[43]

The demise of the manufacturing sector, an important employer for African-American men, has fostered two tiers of income for this group. A few African-American men at the top are faring much better now than in the past, while a larger group at the opposite end of the economic continuum (more than 25 percent) are doing much worse.[44] When layoffs from the manufacturing sector occur, finding a replacement job is more difficult for those clustered at the lower end of the occupational ladder. Worse yet, African-American men, who tend to be clustered at the bottom, are three times as likely as Anglo men to be refused employment.[45] One factor frequently cited by employers as a reason to avoid hiring African-Americans is fear of drug use.[46] The rationale is instructive in that more Anglos than African-Americans are drug users and traffickers.

Lack of human capital is another argument frequently cited to explain the depressed economic situation of African-Americans. However, for those African-Americans who have obtained human capital, the payoff is not the same as it is for their Anglo counterparts. For example, education, which is touted as the great equalizer, brings fewer returns to African-American men (and women) than to Anglos. Sadly, the unemployment rate among college-educated African-American males is four times that of Anglo males. When African-American college graduates obtain a job, they earn only 75 percent as much as Anglo men.[47]

No Job, No Marriage

For African-American men, then, who clearly are at a disadvantage in the marketplace, the marriage market becomes problematic. If marriage is an economic exchange, African-American men have little to offer in the current market. Potential marriage partners, pregnant or not, are unlikely to formalize a union when the prospective mate is unemployed.[48] Similarly, in a study of African-American males, Cliff Johnson and Andrew Sum concluded that a decrease in marriage rates for this group was tied directly to loss of wages.[49] Understandably, marriage is more than twice as likely to occur when an African-American man is employed as when he is not.[50] On the other hand, as marriageable men become more scarce, marriage is delayed, and remarriage is less likely to occur.[51] Even at that, Stier and Tienda found that while the route to marriage for inner-city residents living in poverty is not direct or well paved, a high school diploma or the birth of a child increases the probability of a legal union taking place.[52]

The Resiliency of African-American Families

Despite the political and economic barriers blocking African-Americans over the course of this nation's history, and despite the continuing rhetoric of politicians and social reformers who have declared the African-American family on the verge of extinction, it continues to adapt and survive. Because of the extrafamilial stresses inflicted on African-American families' attempts to be economically independent, family unity often was and continues to be achieved through family members' tenacity and determination. For example, historically, African-American mothers have had to leave their children to the care of extended family or fictive kin on a weekly basis while they tended to the needs of Anglo children. Today, African-American fathers who cannot find a job that will support a spouse and children are often forced to leave their families so that the families can receive government assistance. Under these conditions, African-American (and poor Anglo) fathers live in fear of being found out or reported to a governmental agency if they try to stay in the home with their families. Further, fathers who cannot find employment in the formal economy are compelled to work "off the books," supporting their families surreptitiously. Consequently, more than a hundred years after the end of slavery, African-American families continue to be subjected to disruption, with men forced to be marginal fathers or fathers on the sly.

Some observers, including Wilson, believe that economic assault does far greater damage to African-American families who are poorer now than in the past. Wilson maintains that today African-Americans living in poverty are socially alienated and isolated from African-Americans who have achieved some measure of success and have moved from the poverty-stricken inner city to the suburbs. According to Wilson, when middle-class African-American families fled ghettoized areas, African-Americans living in poverty in the inner city lost the necessary elements for social mobility.[53] They lost role models, an employment network, and access to jobs. They have been left with strapless boots.

The plight of men (Anglo and African-American) is sobering and illuminates what is happening to families. Even at that, it is women who continue to be least able to support their families independently. The distress of women in poverty is the focus of the next section.

THE REALITY FOR FEMALE HEADS OF HOUSEHOLD

The largest proportion of families without homes are unattached women and their children.[54] Much has been written about the "feminization of poverty" recently,[55] but women and children have always fared worse economically than men. Coontz, for example, argues that in an earlier era the sustenance needs of the male head of household commonly took precedence over those of women and children. And if the father departed the household permanently, he was not held legally responsible for supporting his children because he was not there to benefit from their services and wages.[56] In the early part of this century, if one or both parents could not support a child, the child often was placed in an orphanage. As many as 20 percent of children were cared for in this manner. It is instructive that about the same proportion of children live in poverty today, and many of those who do not reside with their families are living with foster families.

Today, as in other time periods, women in the United States are more likely than men to be poor—about 30 percent more likely. Indeed, the United States has a higher gender poverty ratio than many other industrial countries, including the United Kingdom, Canada, Australia, and Italy.[57] In female-headed households, poverty may be due less to the absence of a father figure than to the absence of traditional male earnings—that is, earned income that supports a family's basic needs.[58] Diana Pearce observes that in the 1940s, the median income for female heads of household was 70 percent of married couples' median income. Today it is only 42 percent.[59] The average female annual earnings cap at $22,000 between ages 40 and 44. And at least half of the increase in women's wages relative to men has occurred not through any advances in equality for women, but because of declining real earnings of men.[60] That fact explains in part why one-third of the increase in poverty has occurred in single-parent families.[61]

The same argument that has been offered to explain the wage discrepancy between Anglo and African-American men is reproduced for women. However, table 2.5 illustrates the worth of women's human capital relative to men's. Median income for women with 4 years of college is not much more than the earnings of men with only a high school education. For male college graduates, on the other hand, the median income is $12,000 more than for men with a high school diploma. And women who invest time and energy to obtain human capital in the form of post-graduate training have a median income less than that of males

Table 2.5

Median Annual Income for Year-Round Full-Time Workers Aged 25 and Over, 1990 (Dollars Rounded Off)

Education	Men	Women
<8 years	$17,390	$12,250
4 years high school	26,650	18,320
4 years college	39,240	28,020
5+ college	49,300	33,750

Source: U.S. Department of Education (1992, 391), reprinted in *Women in American Society: An Introduction to Women's Studies* by Virginia Sapiro (Mountain View, Calif.: Mayfield), p. 20.

with only a 4-year degree. Clearly, the payoff for acquiring human capital is not the same for both sexes. Table 2.6 presents women's wages as a proportion of men's and demonstrates that Anglo women who obtain a college degree lose out vis-à-vis Anglo men.

Table 2.6

Women's Wages as a Proportion of Men's Wages, 1990

	4 years of high school	4+ years of college
All Women		
Percent of all men	.55	.64
African-American		
Percent of African-		
American Men	.74	.85
Percent of		
Anglo Men	.54	.68
Anglo		
Percent of		
Anglo Men	.68	.62

Source: Adapted from Census Bureau figures presented in Ms. Foundation for Women (1992). *In Women in American Society: Introduction to Women's Studies* by Virginia Sapiro (Mountain View, Calif.: Mayfield), p. 428.

Like African-American men, African-American women are worse off than their Anglo counterparts. They are more than twice as likely as Anglo women to be unemployed, and almost half who are employed part-time desire full-time work.[62]

Women, Anglo or African-American, trying to support a family, needed to earn a minimum of $14,800 a year in 1991; however, part-time work of 25 hours a week at minimum wage yielded about $5,100 in gross earnings.[63] The average amount received in Aid to

Families With Dependent Children transfer payments, including food stamps and Medicaid, is equivalent to a wage of $5.15 per hour. Then there are the additional costs a working mother incurs that a mother receiving AFDC does not. According to Kathryn Edin, a mid-1980s survey concluded that working mothers spend about $2,800 per year on child care, clothing, transportation, and health care.[64] When women forsake the shaky security of AFDC to work at minimum wage, they risk financial disaster as well as a possible loss of housing for themselves and their children. It is evident from Table 2.7 that the majority of child care occurs in someone's home, either by husband, wife, another relative, or a nonrelative. Only about a third of child care is arranged through an organized day care center. Lack of affordable available child care is a consistent problem for families. It is instructive that the United States and South Africa are the only industrialized societies that do not have national day care for their citizens. On the other hand, in France, public nursery schools are available for all children age three and over, with 100 percent participation.[65] And in Sweden,

Table 2.7

Child-Care Arrangements for Children Younger than 5 Years of Age, 1990

Setting	Percent
Relatives	27
Family	20
Child's home (nonrelative)	6
Day care center	38
Other	9

Source: The State of America's Children 1992 (Washington, D.C.: Children's Defense Fund), p. 17.

one parent can take up to 30 months off work to care for a newborn and receive 90 percent of her/his pay. After the 30-month period, public child care is available for parents who need it.[66] The bottom line is that men are finding it increasingly difficult to be the sole support of their families. And even though more and more women are working to support families, too many families are on a downward spiral. The statistics about families' economic circumstances indicate that the rhetoric of politicians and some social scientists is misguided and off the mark. Families are not lacking values so much as they are lacking economic stability.

Part II

THE SOCIAL PSYCHOLOGICAL EXPERIENCE OF POVERTY AND SHELTER LIFE

Chapter 3

Shelter Life and Women's Self-Concept

In his study of people without permanent housing, Michael Sosin noted that while many have never held a job, there is evidence that the majority have worked at some point in time. Most worked at blue-collar jobs in early adulthood and then had long periods of irregular and sporadic employment. Still others managed to subsist with some form of income maintenance at some time.[1]

The fact that the majority have had income indicates that whatever the precipitating factor, being without a home is not a sudden event for most people. Typically, the loss of one's home follows a downward spiral that exhausts family savings, support from relatives and friends, and often social service resources.[2] Those without homes do not necessarily lack social ties. On the other hand, they may be uninformed about the process or procedure for tapping benefits to escape their predicament.[3] Having examined in chapter 2 the multiplicity of structural variables that are operating in the lives of those who are poor, we now turn attention to the socioemotional cost of being without permanent housing.

LIFE IN TEMPORARY SHELTERS

How far has society progressed in caring for persons in poverty or without homes? We can respond smugly that at least we no longer lock the poor and the mentally ill in poorhouses, as we did in the past. We are more humane in our treatment. We support rehabilitation for the poor to some extent, but preferably at no cost to us personally or collectively.

Today, near the end of the twentieth century, temporary shelters are society's primary response to those who have no place to live. Generally organized by not-for-profit social service agencies, shelters have received both criticism and praise for giving people a temporary home. Even shelter administrators, however, recognize the problems created by temporary housing.

As part of this study I interviewed the director, staff, and women who were former guests of Hope House. During my interviews with former shelter guests, several women expressed frustration about a system that requires that people lose most of their material possessions before they can receive assistance. Describing their feelings of powerlessness when no agency would listen to their pleas for assistance until they had been forced from their homes, the women's emotional tone indicated that their plight, rather than dismissed from their memory, left a residue of anguish.

Although it costs less to stabilize a family's living arrangements while they are in their home than when they are without a home, many, if not most, agency rent-assistance programs require an eviction notice preceding monetary help. Former shelter guests expressed frustration about not being granted housing assistance until they were evicted, in a shelter, and able to enlist the support of the Hope House staff. The women insisted that they were not ignorant or naive about the process of helping themselves, as the literature suggests. Rather, they felt ignored and unheard. One woman said it made her furious, but she knew that if she emoted fury, no caseworker would help her. Tragically, the women's assessment of their situation is on target. Some scholars, such as Margaret Wilkerson and Jewell Gresham, maintain that often the inhumane treatment by various government workers and/or social service agencies is the most traumatizing of all problems endured by people in poverty.[4]

Certainly the social environment for those without homes is a maze of welfare offices, food stamp offices, social service agencies, the legal system, the school system, and the community at large. Rigid governmental and/or social service regulations that impair family stability add stress to already strained familial relationships. Adult family members feel constrained in their ability to conduct their personal affairs. Imagine yourself in the predicament of needing assistance. You are a high school dropout with underdeveloped verbal and written skills and lacking social skills. You feel degraded because you are an adult and you have to ask for help to support your family—a job society says you should do yourself. At every agency that you approach for assistance, strangers ask you personal questions about your income, your parenting ability, housing, food, alcohol, drugs, sexual abuse, physical abuse. The list seems endless. You try not to appear defensive. You know you must cooperate if you are to secure help. You are compelled to tell intimate details of your life to stranger after stranger. You feel there is no personal privacy left.

Former shelter guests recalled their anger and frustration when other agencies required a "credible" person (a Hope House worker) to intervene on the client's behalf. The word "humiliated" was used often by these women to describe their feelings, especially when relating that the explanations they offered about their housing and economic situation were not sufficient to obtain assistance. These women felt outrage that someone else had to vouch for the authenticity of their experience. Although the staff members believed that in many cases clients were hindered by their inability to communicate their needs clearly and cogently, they supported the women's claim that agencies do not always "hear" the clients' voices.

It is a conundrum. The roots of social work as a profession run deep in the pursuit of systemic change, but frequently social work practitioners come to the profession to "help people," not to alter structural patterns. And yet those who seek assistance too often view social workers not as helpers but as agents of an oppressive system that distrusts and maligns those who are living in poverty. The women experienced dual feelings of blame and shame.

A GOFFMANIAN PERSPECTIVE

Erving Goffman's analysis of a mental asylum is useful in interpreting guests' ambivalent experience of shelter life. Goffman argues that upon entering an asylum, patients bring in the culture of their life outside.[5] The same can be said of shelter guests. They arrive with their own values, habits, and customs, which differ from shelter norms. In both the asylum and the shelter, the individual arrives with a self-concept based on experiences outside the institution—a self-concept that has been formed and altered throughout their lives. In both the shelter and the institution, those who enter are subjected (intentionally or not) to behavior modification that erodes their previous self-image. Writers on this topic maintain that all too often, shelter staff members exhibit a middle-class, Anglo value system that disposes them to do battle with the "culture of poverty" they encounter at the door of the shelter.[6]

Goffman's description of the "mortification process," his term for a patient's experience in a mental institution, differs little from anything a guest in a shelter might undergo: "The self that existed prior to institution [shelter] is defined as having been in some way the cause of the patient's [guest's] present condition. The old self must be destroyed, and a new self incorporated through a resocialization process."[7]

Hope House shelter director Jamie Mayerson and her staff were disturbed by the suggestion that shelters are akin to total institutions such as mental hospitals. Ms. Mayerson and the shelter personnel view their work differently. In many ways they feel that staff members act as role models and agents for positive change for the women who come to the shelter. Far from viewing guests' values as deviating dramatically from their own, they believe that their clients' situation stems from several factors, including difficulty in setting priorities for their needs, inexperience in developing realistic short-term goals, and inability to follow a process to achieve those goals.

A major obstacle to goal setting for those who are poor is that their needs for food, shelter, and clothing have not been met. Energy and effort necessary for pursuing long-term goals and objectives is spent in pursuing short-term material needs. Ms. Mayerson and her staff believe that their work with shelter guests affects many areas of their guests' life, from setting priorities for responsibilities to disciplining children, in essence, resocialization.

One staff member referred to case management as "front-loading"—intense, short-term resocialization that can have long-term consequences. Staff members view this process as introducing a sense of order into lives that have become chaotic and lack predictability because of poverty circumstances.

When I interviewed former guests, they expressed a combination of frustration and relief about their stay in a shelter. They recalled what they believed to be rigid rules for personal cleanliness, housekeeping chores, discipline, mealtimes, and bedtime. Some researchers, such as Timmer, Eitzen, and Talley, support their perceptions, arguing that shelters all too often value rule enforcement over emotional support.[8] Recognizing the dissonance that occurs between house rules and guests' unique routines, Hope House shelter staff members attempt to include guests' input into shelter issues that affect their immediate circumstances. However, just as with Goffman's asylum inmates, the guests understand who has legitimate authority to make the rules and who is supposed to comply.

Again, like patients in a mental institution, guests in a shelter often feel they have little control over their lives. Generally they respond in one of several ways: by withdrawing, accommodating, being converted, or resisting.[9] Because living on the street is tantamount to neglect, most women who seek refuge in a shelter for themselves and their children accommodate and acquiesce, fearing the loss of their children if they do not comply. Thus the hopelessness and powerlessness that they experience when losing their housing are exacerbated by the limits on the control they feel they can safely exert in a shelter. In other words, the women follow the rules so as not to jeopardize losing their children or failing to find a home for them.

According to interviews with former shelter guests, accommodation appears to be the most common strategy utilized to survive the system. Even at that, staff noted that guests display some resistance to the Goffmanian aspects of shelter life, such as bureaucratic and administrative shelter rules and regulations, organizational statuses and roles that they fear might usurp prior familial roles, lack of privacy and personal space, and absence of autonomy—characteristics that anyone would resist.

The women recalled feeling an overwhelming sense of powerlessness and a lack of control upon entering shelter. They feared eviction or worse if their resistance appeared too strong. Keenly aware that shelter staff members had the influence and the connections to help them obtain housing—something they could not accomplish themselves outside the shelter—the women seemed to feel that accommodation was a small price to pay.

EXTENDED STAYS IN SHELTER

Causes and Consequences

Because low-income housing is in short supply and because cash is necessary for moving into stable housing, shelter stays are increasingly extended. Further, because Hope House (like many shelters for women and children) does not accept males over age 12, family members can be separated for several months at a time. Prolonging the resolution of their housing situation compounds family members' stress and anxiety, and interferes with parents' and children's ability to interact within a normative familial framework.

Fathers, who may already feel marginal to the family unit because of their inability to protect their family as the culture dictates, can become increasingly alienated from their wives and children staying in a shelter. Mothers fare no better. Chafing under poverty and isolated from their partners, they must carry the burden of parenting alone, all the while under the watchful eye of strangers who they believe control their fate.

Depression in Shelter Guests

Ms. Mayerson reported that several years ago the average stay in the shelter was two weeks; now it frequently lasts months. She added that the longer it takes to find permanent housing for a family, the more likely that symptoms of mental depression will be evident in the women and children. And the longer the stay, the more profound the symptoms of the depression. One staff member, recalling her experiences with many of the women guests, said that women seem almost buoyant during the initial interview because of their hope that the agency will obtain housing for them immediately. When the search becomes protracted, however, the women grow increasingly quiet, distant, and withdrawn. Staff members described the guests as expressionless, flat, almost masklike in appearance.

This depression serves at least two purposes. First, by internalizing their rage rather than expressing it outwardly, shelter guests can appear to be coping and in control—characteristics that are rewarded in our society. Because guests rely on the assistance of agency personnel to help with their housing, it is to their benefit to maintain a demeanor acceptable to those in charge. Second, from a sociological perspective, internalized anger lessens the likelihood that the social order will be disrupted.

Shelter life makes for a tenuous social order. At Hope House, the presence of thirty women and children or more living in crowded circumstances with little private space is hardly conducive to peaceful coexistence or consensus building. Some observers, including Bonnie Hausman and Constance Hammen,[10] maintain that staying in shelter interferes with a mother's parental role by increasing her feelings of incompetency regarding the familial role. The staff members, aware that the shelter stay exaggerates this sense of incompetency, attempt to develop empowerment strategies for the women in their care.

For example, although predetermined housekeeping tasks must be done, the shelter guests decide who does what and when. The women with whom I spoke indicated that they complied and cooperated for the most part with staff. Some of the women viewed their work as payment for room and board, especially having been made aware that the agency was underfunded and understaffed. The women felt an obligation to assist with the maintenance, but they said they did not feel empowered.

Perhaps a more critical form of empowerment is the staff's attempts to put in place a system that allows shelter guests and their children to settle disputes that arise among mothers and children. Because of a mother's anguish about the uncertainty of her family's housing situation and the lack of familial privacy in a shelter, it is not unusual for interpersonal conflict to erupt. As much as is feasible, shelter staff members encourage the mothers to negotiate disagreements that arise among families and within families. Staff hope to resolve conflict, and perhaps more important to build community among the families.

Even with the best of intentions and the most highly skilled staff, the lack of a home and life in temporary housing often have severe, sustained consequences for the women's self-concept. The trauma occurs not necessarily because of any failure of the shelter staff, who recognize and address the issues that guests bring to the shelter, but because our system failed them long ago, long before they arrived at shelter.

Chapter 4

Shelter Life and Its Effects on Children's Development

What are children who live in poverty, in substandard housing, and in unsafe neighborhoods to believe of a society that claims to revere the family and to hold family values superior to all other values? How does temporary housing affect children?

Children who live in a transitional state know no structure, no order, no predictability; they know only chaos.[1] For a child who looks to the adults in her life for security, the sight of her mother or father losing control over life's basic needs can damage her development of trust and sense of security. Many factors can influence the impact of such a transitional state, including the length of time in which the family is without a home, the availability of a support system for the family, and the child's age, sex, and temperament. Even so, the child is influenced by the emotional and physical environment of the available temporary housing.[2]

Loss of home is not the only event that affects a child's sense of security. The process of poverty begins with one or a combination of crises, including separation, divorce, or death of a parent or caretaker, the head of household's loss of employment, declining household income, loss of extended-kin support system, and/or increased family conflict. Any of these factors can affect a child profoundly, and in combination they can have long-term consequences for a child's emotional and physical development. Children require a nurturing, supportive, caring, safe, predictable home life in order to thrive and acquire a sense of self-worth, and a lack of a permanent home disrupts that process.[3]

The institutional environment of a shelter can heighten the crisis of an already tenuous familial relationship and compound the trauma experienced by a child without a home. A parent who is feeling powerless and helpless because of the family's situation is emotionally unable to reassure a frightened child, whose feelings mirror those of the parent.[4] Children typically subjected to conflicting behavior expectations from mothers and staff become overwhelmed and confused. Their anxiety is heightened, not alleviated, by shelter life.[5]

When a child remains largely uncomforted and insecure, she is more likely to exhibit any of an array of maladaptive behaviors, including depression, aggressiveness, restlessness, regressive behavior, hyperactivity, and anxiety. The child's sense of self is traumatized. There is some evidence that the emotional assault that is entwined with being without a permanent space negatively affects a child's expectations about his or her future.[6]

Frequent changes in home environment, structure, and neighborhood can affect a child's sense that she belongs to some place and that some place belongs to her—the child's personal space or turf. Although the environment lacks permanence, one factor that generally remains constant for children living in poverty is the ghettoization of their lives. Typically, any area that they call home has been abandoned by the more affluent and is isolated from the economically vibrant portions of the city.

POOR CHILDREN AND SCHOOLS

For children without a home, school could be a "haven in a heartless world." The few hours a day these children spend at school might well be the only time when they enjoy a sense of order or predictability.[7] Even so, feelings of insecurity and inferiority surrounding these children's home lives can harm them in various areas, including formation of friendships, schoolwork, and attendance. Children who have stayed in a shelter spoke of the ridicule they encountered because of their situation. They coped in various ways. Sometimes they feigned illness to avoid going to school and facing the other children. Another tactic was to get off the school bus before their stop at the shelter so the other children would not see them enter their "home." Children described the pain of being stigmatized by classmates, who frequently taunted them because of their temporary residence.

Unfortunately, some teachers' treatment of the children can be as callous as the taunting by their schoolmates. Often teachers view the issues that children without homes, who live in poverty, bring to the classroom as interfering with teaching. Because any negative reaction on the part of classmates and/or teacher heightens the child's sense of alienation, the child might feel the need to become secretive, protective, and deceptive about her or his personal life.[8] The more often the child employs these defense mechanisms, the more isolated she will be.

Thus life can be a catch-22 for a child without a home. The more she attempts to keep her family situation secret, the more distrusted, suspect, and marginalized she becomes. The most effective way to keep the family secret is to play truant; one study found that 43 percent of school-age children who lacked a permanent home did not attend school. For many children, then, especially adolescents, dropping out is the solution.[9]

Education: Not an Equalizer

Frequently the desperate day-to-day life of poor children and their parents clashes with the educational system. Pierre Bordieu's perspective on education explains the disadvantaged position of poor children in the classroom. Children living in poverty experience the world at a primitive level. Their parents exhaust their psychic energy in search of life's basic needs—food, shelter, and clothing. These children and their families live a concrete existence and speak concrete language about problems relating to their survival. However, the culture of education, disseminated through abstract concepts, presupposes that children have transcended the concrete, essentials of life. Teachers assume that children are prepared for conceptualizing, but children living in poverty generally are not. They have not had the luxury of experiencing abstract ways of thinking. The progressive nature of schoolwork is a constant struggle for them. Bordieu's thinking underscores the point that children living in poverty are excluded from the language and culture of education, and further, that the educational system, portrayed as neutral, is laden with the ideas of the elite.[10] Bordieu's perspective would explain the dropout rate of children in poverty and/or without homes as well as the high proportion of working class and poor children in vocational classes. The language of vocational coursework is familiar. Only 29 percent of children who are poor are placed in the college preparatory track, compared with 65 percent of students from high-income families.[11]

Without a conceptual understanding of their world, the probability intensifies that poor children will be left out of the school curriculum and instruction. Equally important, because of their situation, they risk being excluded from most circles of friends. Thus over time they resort to the most effective exclusion, self-exclusion, which severely decreases their chances for upward mobility.[12] Current research on intergenerational mobility provides evidence supporting the assertion that children whose parents belong to today's underclass have a higher than average probability of taking their parents' place as adults.[13]

The McKinney Act of 1987 mandated that children without homes are entitled to receive an education like all other children. In response to the mandate, the state of Kentucky formed Family Resource Centers in schools in which the majority of students are at or below poverty level. The resource centers facilitate children's attendance in school by assisting them with material needs such as clothing, food, and school supplies, and nonmaterial needs such as counseling and tutoring. In addition, Family Resource Center staff members emphasize to parents the importance of parental involvement with a child's education and encourage parents to volunteer in some way at school. Personnel at the resource center attempt to work with school faculty members to encourage parental involvement. In an interview with a former staff member at a northern Kentucky resource center, however, I learned that school faculty members often do not encourage involvement on the part of these parents. Mothers with whom I spoke told of feeling welcome at the resource center, but not in other areas of the school, especially as classroom mothers. Each mother who had attempted to become an assistant in the classroom told of the teacher's lack of encouragement for the parent's participation. One mother told of an experience where she repeatedly volunteered to assist the teacher while the teacher never asked the mother to assist. Further, the mother maintained that the teacher seemed irritated every time the mother volunteered for classroom activities.

Again, from Bordieu's perspective, teachers typically bring middle-class value systems to education. If they are ill equipped to cope with children living in poverty, their judgment of the children's parents is likely to be even less tolerant, less emphatic, less accepting. Indeed, it would be anathema for classrooms laden with middle-class ideology and for the teachers in those classrooms to view a mother who receives AFDC as a potential role model for the students.

If children of parents who are poor and without housing are to reach even half (national test scores indicate many are not achieving even half) of their potential in school, educators must go beyond legal mandates. Flexible school systems and empathic teachers are needed for coping with children's socioeconomic and sociocultural diversity.

Unwelcoming School Structures

Unfortunately, the forbidding atmosphere of school buildings in poor neighborhoods can and does reinforce negative messages that poor children receive from the educational system. Antiquated structures, peeling paint, crumbling plaster, and restrooms in constant disrepair tell children they are unimportant. Children learn a lesson that is as lasting as any classroom instruction, if not more so: not to expect much from any situation they enter. For these children, the atmosphere at school is consistent with the atmosphere at home. They grow up believing that this is all there is, this is all they can expect in life, and this is all they deserve.

As middle-class families continue to flee inner-city school systems, the quality of education in those systems has little chance of improving. Because the proportion of households with children in public schools continues to decrease (currently it is about 24 percent), school levies cannot easily muster support. Increasingly, school systems heavily populated by poor Anglos and members of minorities have fewer resources for basic instructional materials. Poor children are the initial losers, but eventually the whole society loses. Taking care of all children early in their lives is a cost-effective investment; certainly it is less costly to society than rehabilitating or incarcerating adults.

THE ROLE OF THE COMMUNITY ENVIRONMENT

Research has established a relationship between dilapidated, economically deprived communities and maladaptive childhood development.[14] Yet there is evidence that even a homogeneous, poor neighborhood can provide children with a buffer against some of the stressors of poverty. Because children living in a totally poor environment are not likely to be in contact with children who enjoy greater material comfort, their self-esteem is less likely to become bruised. They are less likely to be judged by appearances.

Athletic competition frequently brings together children who are disparate in income and race or ethnicity. Differences between lower-income neighborhood schools and middle-income suburban schools are discerned easily in the neighborhood setting, the age and condition of the structure, the quality of the gymnasium, and the team uniforms. Thus even seemingly innocuous athletic meetings have the potential to affect the self-concept of students from schools in poor communities.

On the other hand, children who interact exclusively with persons in their poverty-ridden communities run the risk of adopting characteristics of their neighborhood role models. Two of the children interviewed for this study, sisters aged 9 and 11, spoke matter-of-factly about living in an apartment building in which drug dealers also lived. They recalled the fear they felt when they saw a SWAT (Special Weapons and Tactics) team surround their building in order to apprehend the traffickers. They also reported that the police did not bother to verify whether other tenants were present in the building. Normal police procedure should include ensuring the safety of those in the vicinity of a potentially dangerous arrest. One study suggests that 38 percent of youngsters aged 10 to 17 fear that they could be hurt by someone using drugs.[15] Children should not have to fear being injured by police who are in pursuit of those suspected of committing a crime. Are safety procedures routinely ignored in lower-income neighborhoods? Besides the obvious physical risk to children living among drug dealers, there is the danger that deviance will become normalized in their minds. Children living in such conditions become acutely sensitive to deviance and develop a high tolerance. The sisters giggled, for example, when they described the drug dealers as kind, generous men who gave neighborhood children candy, money, and motorcycle rides. Perhaps it is to their advantage that they did not fully grasp the immediate danger or the long-term consequences of their circumstances. Yet occasional face-to-face encounters with others outside their community, whose lifestyle is very different, might not be the solution. It might simply emphasize the inequities.

Bringing Order to Unordered Lives

Because the lives of children in poverty and those without housing are out of control, they often fight for control in any arena they enter, such as the classroom, the school playground, the football field, or the gymnasium.[16] In a society that reveres the home, children without a home soon learn from their environment—their classmates, television, films, and the print media—that their situation is considered abnormal and undesirable. And as these children progress through adolescence—these children who have never been allowed to be children, and who live in a society where middle- and upper-class children are idolized and overindulged by their parents—some rebel against their parents, some vandalize their own community, and some choose the safest victims for destruction: themselves. Those who survive childhood will take their place at the lower levels of the class structure, believing that they will achieve parity with those in other social classes if they only work harder and longer. The great majority will never do so.

According to Charles Cooley's "looking glass" theory, which maintains that we see ourselves reflected in the eyes of others,[17] children who lack permanent housing are likely to see themselves as undesirable. Depending on the child's age, temperament, and familial relationships, he or she will develop protective coping mechanisms such as extreme introversion (as in withdrawal) or extreme extroversion (as in acting out in various ways such as aggressive behavior).[18]

Staff members at Hope House have experienced a variety of coping strategies on the part of children. They stated that age is a factor in determining behavior. Older children who could comprehend the total picture were embarrassed about the situation and the lack of privacy; they tended to withdraw. Younger children, who could not verbalize their insecurity, tended to cling to their mothers. Still others, who sensed their mothers' loss of power over them in the shelter, became disruptive.

CHILDREN AND SHELTER LIFE

Despite the best efforts on the part of an excellent shelter like Hope House, staff members acknowledge that the artificial home environment cannot replace the stabilizing, secure effect of permanent housing for children and their parents. If the familiar constantly gives way to the unfamiliar, a child often ceases to form attachments to people and places. This behavior pattern affects performance of adult roles and places the next generation at risk.[19]

The two sisters introduced earlier discussed the difficulty of adapting to shelter life, in which they had lived for 3½ months. Within the shelter, the most troublesome features were sharing their room with another family and the resulting lack of privacy. Another issue (less serious but nonetheless irritating) was the abundance of rules in the shelter: rules that contradicted their way of life outside the shelter, rules for minor things such as snacks in the evening or doing homework at a specified time, rules for everything.

One mother told of her preadolescent son's crying spells. He, his mother, and a younger sibling had to share a room with a family with adolescent girls. Although he had little contact with the girls, sharing a room with strangers was experienced as a tremendous loss of control in his life. He had a sense of dread and mortification about the possibilities the situation presented. Changing his clothes became a battle for the mother because he was afraid the girls would walk in on him. He was fearful, too, of having his few possessions taken. One can only imagine the lifelong consequences for this traumatized child.

Outside the shelter, a major concern for children was hiding their shelter life. The sisters described the measures they took to keep their "home" a secret from their classmates. They made certain that none of their schoolmates ever saw them enter or leave the shelter. Ridicule from classmates who knew they were staying in a shelter was one of their most painful experiences. Former shelter guests confirmed the girls' perceptions and observed that their adolescent children were mortified about their temporary residence. Even at that, not all their experiences with the shelter were negative. The girls spoke positively about some of their shelter experiences. Looking surprised by their own admission, they happily reported that their mother could not whip them when they disobeyed, as was her custom. The girls also pointed out that as shelter guests, they were offered recreational opportunities that would not have been available. Some of the amenities included tickets to concerts and ball games donated by local corporations. A favorite activity was going to the local Boys and Girls Club for swimming and other activities.

An agency in the role of the good provider presents a double-edged sword for families in shelter. Parents, by definition, are supposed to be the providers of the good things in life, including recreational events for children. Parents living in poverty cannot indulge their children in costly leisure activities. Therefore, when an agency replaces the parents as provider, mothers expressed mixed emotions. They were happy to see their children enjoying the event, but they also felt saddened about their inability to be the one making their child's life more enjoyable. It threatened their status as a parent. Perhaps one of the hardest things for us to understand about those living in poverty is their seeming lack of gratitude for works of charity and philanthropy. It is difficult to comprehend that dependency breeds hostility, not gratitude. Most people, given the choice, would choose independence over being on the receiving end of charity.

Familial Relationships in Shelters

When asked about the familial relationships that shelter guests reveal to case managers, Ms. Mayerson and the staff responded without hesitation and almost in unison. Recounting frequent observations of blurred boundaries between mothers and children, they said, "Parents do not parent, and children are not children." Childhood appears to be lost for the youngsters they see. The eldest child or the older children frequently serve as caretakers for the parent as well as the younger children. Although daughters are more likely to be caregivers for all others, staff members reported that typically the sons act like adult male partners for their mothers. Mothers rely on their sons as a wife would rely on a husband. Staff members also pointed out that it was not uncommon for mothers to sleep with their preteen sons (as noted in chapter 3, males over age 12 may not stay at Hope House).

Although the mother-child relationships observed by workers seemed to be outside normative expectations from a sociological perspective, a mother's reliance on her children can be understood in several ways. First, from a material standpoint, mothers existing at a survival level have a vague notion of the current cultural prescriptions for performing the mother role, but they have little hope of enacting it. These women have no home, no money, no food, few belongings, and no support system that offers them sustained protection.

Second, the women and their children exhibit vestiges of paradigmatic kin relationships of other eras. For example, families living in poverty resemble members of hunting-and-gathering societies but lack the security and community of a kinship group. The children, like the young of hunting-and-gathering societies, who assisted with sustenance as soon as they could take their place in the group, forage with and sometimes substitute for their parents. Contemporary children whose parents cannot provide for them adequately are producers as well as consumers, like the children of the hunters and gatherers.

Further, families in poverty reflect medieval times, when boundaries between childhood and adulthood hardly existed. During that period, children were treated like small adults (but without the privileges), and took on the roles of caretaker and provider at very young ages.[20] Young boys assumed men's responsibilities; if the father died or departed, the son acted as head of the family. Because housing was scarce and living space inadequate for the poor in the burgeoning cities of that time (just as they are now), family members frequently slept together.

Families living in poverty today cannot be expected to exhibit twentieth-century middle-class Western norms. Earlier models of family and kinship groups might provide more useful explanations of their existence than the current cultural paradigms of motherhood and parenthood. The latter appear almost irrelevant to the material conditions in which these families find themselves.

We must not assume that such behavior is limited to poor persons and those without homes. We do not know the extent to which the familial relationships revealed to workers in shelters are unique to the guest population and to what extent they reflect the larger society. Certainly the research does not support the conclusion that "deviant" familial behavior is the exclusive domain of the poor. The evidence indicates that maladaptive treatment of children, including incest, cuts across all income levels but too often escapes attention unless the family is forced into public scrutiny for some reason. Families are subjected to public examination, for example, when they apply for assistance with income, housing, and/or food. Although behavior bordering on the incestuous is not to be condoned, we cannot assume that incest is class bound or that it is the cause or the consequence of the circumstances surrounding families without homes.

Deviance of any kind is more likely to be uncovered among persons seeking income assistance than among other families, because higher-income families generally can avoid confrontations with an intrusive legal system. The once-private lives of families who seek federal, state, or local assistance are subjected to scrutiny by numerous strangers. Often such families are asked repeatedly to explain their income and budgetary actions, their lifestyle, and their parenting techniques.

Hope House staff members have been trained to understand and accept the uniqueness of each family's situation. While staying alert to behavior that could harm the children, they work with families without passing judgment. They know the realities of shelter guests' lives and remain alert to their self-conscious struggle to achieve the status of the "normative American family."

SOCIETAL RESPONSE TO THOSE WITHOUT HOMES

Our society's response to the growing numbers of people without homes has been ill conceived. It is almost too little, too late. Policies supporting temporary shelter as a solution are based on the assumption that individuals' and families' housing problems are temporary and that people need only a brief stay in a shelter to regain economic solvency. Yet systemic factors beyond individuals' control, such as a shortage of full-time jobs, increased part-time and temporary service work, declining wages, a decrease in affordable housing, and cuts in federal and state assistance for families, have contributed to a crisis-based way of life for increasing numbers of people. Because of unfavorable economic conditions, temporary shelters have become more than a one-time respite; they are a recurring reality for more and more lower-income individuals and families. The dismantling of federal welfare programs that is about to begin means that the chronic crisis living conditions of poor families will reach epidemic proportions.[21] Temporary housing has not been enough. What will happen when federal funding is completely gone?

Part III

SOLUTIONS: SOME OLD, SOME NEW

Chapter 5

A Solution for Shrinking Funds: Mandated Community Collaboration

It is doubtful that more than a small percentage of people in this country are aware that the federal share of welfare amounts to only 1 percent of the more than $1.3 trillion federal budget, or that the average state share amounts to less than 3.5 percent. One might ask, if such meager proportions of the federal and state budgets are targeted for welfare, why the emphasis on the topic by candidates? One might further speculate that if constituents availed themselves of information about how federal and state budgets are apportioned, they would seek greater accountability from their representatives about the remaining 96 to 99 percent of the budgetary pie. Instead, declining family values, absent fathers, and fathers who do not support their families financially have become the focus of political debates and media editorials.

By castigating fathers, the issue of poverty is reduced to the individual level by politicians, thereby absolving society of responsibility for children living without homes. While the diatribe rages and intensifies in election years, more and more children are born and raised in temporary housing, enter school at a disadvantage, drop out of school, work at minimum-wage jobs or not at all, and give birth to the next generation of children in temporary housing.

NEW SOLUTIONS, OLD PROBLEMS

Because governing bodies at the state and federal levels continue to commit fewer revenues to domestic human services, not-for-profit agencies are scrambling for the diminished pot. In light of declining dollars, federal and state human service components are increasingly mandating community-based collaborative initiatives to address the growing population slipping into poverty. Simply put, more people are falling over the edge and less and increasingly less monies are available to assist. From this emergent rational model for not-for-profits, social services are directed to operate like for-profit corporations. Operations are to be consumer driven, and efficiency dictates no duplication of services for at-risk individuals and family. Just as in the for-profit arena, not-for-profits are expected to use their dollars effectively and efficiently.

Because of the Republicans' contract with America, President Clinton's endorsement of the abolishment of welfare—which spells the end of federal spending for the poor—and the general fiscal climate emerging out of Washington, the onus will be on states to help those in need. Some states, like Kentucky, have seen the hand-writing on the wall and are pursuing methods to make their monies targeted for human services stretch further. Grants increasingly are awarded to local services that are part of an integrated community network. Perhaps more important, funding will target prevention and early intervention for individuals and families.[1] Although many, if not most, social service providers already have loosely knit networks of care in place to provide mutual assistance on behalf of clients, in the past competition for limited funds kept agencies from forging formal partnerships. Now, however, the collaboration directive propels agencies to jointly pursue funding.

In theory, partnerships between service providers and nonduplication of services should benefit targeted populations—those without homes and those on the brink of losing their homes. However, congressional proposals to reduce that portion of the federal budget that is allocated for human services for both children and the elderly would impair the ability of collaborative initiatives to aid those in poverty.

A Case Study of Collaboration

At Hope House, an interagency cooperative effort was developed and underwritten by a 3 year grant from the Department of Health and Human Services. The case managers interviewed for this study unanimously agreed that forming a network with community service providers benefited clients. Within the framework of a program called "Stabilization," each case manager at Hope House becomes the coordinator of services for a client in what is called a "continuum of care." As the coordinator, the case manager initiates services in the community (as well as in-agency services) for the client, and acts as the primary contact person for all other agencies involved with the client's care. If a client needs psychological counseling, for example, the case manager refers her to a counselor who has an interagency agreement to give Hope House clients priority service. In this way, multiple service providers work synergistically on behalf of a client.

The Stabilization program is designed to steady families; that is, to lessen the economic, physical, and emotional fluctuation of people who are at risk of being without a home for any number of reasons. Based on the notion that prevention-intervention is not only cost effective in terms of dollars but also in terms of a client's sense of self, it operates on the premise that building on an individual's strengths is more productive than focusing on a person's weaknesses. Like shelter staff, Stabilization personnel believe that clients' values do not deviate dramatically from the mainstream simply because they are living in poverty. Rather, clients are perceived as lacking the basic tools to obtain some of society's resources.

The major function of intervention-prevention programs like Stabilization is to intervene before the downward momentum toward losing the family home and other pieces of family life becomes unstoppable. Otherwise, the situation becomes more difficult to reverse for the family. Stabilizing families allows them to take preliminary steps in the direction of financial equilibrium. Stabilization provides the basis for progress toward quasi-economic independence.

Case Managers as Advocates, Not Parents

Case managers at Hope House maintain that the process of stabilizing families and individuals departs from what social work typically offers—paternalism at best, effete snobbism at worse. Rather than taking the role of a finger-pointing parent or an "if you could just adopt my values" approach, the Stabilization program seeks to forge a case manager-client partnership. The program espouses the development of a relationship of mutuality and empowerment, not dependency. In this way, the articulation of a staff member's education and social work experience and a client's life experience occurs. Ideally, on the premise that a client understands best what changes must occur in his or her life, the case manager acts as the client's coach, trainer, and even cheerleader to facilitate change.

Jocelyn Carrington, executive director of Hope House, believes that those of us not experiencing the ravages of poverty can learn much about survival from those living in poverty. She asks, "How many of us could survive on $228.00 dollars a month for ourselves and two children" as mothers receiving AFDC in Kentucky are expected to do? According to Ms. Carrington, clients are ongoing teachers about life and the harsh reality of poverty. In fact, she feels that neophyte social workers are and should be first and foremost students of clients. Effective social workers must learn to listen empathetically in order to fully understand the needs of those in poverty. The difficulty is that they must do so without becoming enablers. In the process Ms. Carrington believes case managers learn to appreciate and draw upon clients' assets rather than focus on their deficiencies.

A major advantage of a prevention-intervention human services model is that it is less detrimental to familial roles than the traditional emergency or crisis-driven model of assistance. Mothers, fathers, and their children avoid the humiliation of eviction, the possibility of losing what little furniture they might possess, and the final degradation of seeking temporary housing in a shelter. Monetarily, it is less costly to everyone involved—family, landlord, social service agencies, and government agencies.

The "Cents" of Intervention

It is estimated that preventing a family from losing a home cost about 15 percent less (a savings of $1,140) than the cost of sheltering a family for one month.[2] Many who are without a home left because the landlord told them to leave, perhaps in a heated argument over deficiencies in the apartment or because of a late payment, but most do not leave because of a formal eviction process. And between one-third and one-half of those who receive an eviction notice simply depart the apartment or residence without responding to the notice or without contacting the landlord to mediate the problem. It is believed that perhaps as many as half of those who are without homes would not have lost their homes if a formal or informal eviction process had been halted. Fewer than 15 percent of those without a home had received a formal eviction, and barely a fourth of those who had received an eviction notice sought some form of assistance in response. Yet Eric Lindblom found that when faced with formal eviction, 58 percent of tenants who obtained legal counsel won, as opposed to only 6 percent of those who did not seek legal representation.

Through programs like Stabilization, case managers strategize with clients about mediating with landlords. In coaching clients about their rights and responsibilities as tenants, they offer alternative problem-solving techniques for rental disputes.

Because a formal eviction incurs costs in time and, perhaps more important to landlords, money—court fees, attorney fees, apartment cleanup, and repairs—it is in a landlord's monetary interest to negotiate with a nonpaying tenant. There is evidence that when landlords consent to work with a tenant, they are reasonably sure of receiving their money. In New York City, for example, an eviction prevention program saved $3.3 million in local, state, and federal funds for housing assistance during one 18-month period.[3]

Housing Pacts Program

A strategy developed by Hope House to prevent eviction is the Housing Pacts Program (HPP). The program is designed to form partnerships between Hope House and local tenement and apartment building owners. One component of the program offers landlords the option of direct rent payments, direct utility payments, and flexible rental agreements. In exchange, the landlord agrees to work with the tenant and Hope House to avoid an eviction or accept a client as a new tenant (one the landlord might have refused without the partnership with Hope House). Under the agreement, a participating client's check is mailed to Hope House, and the case manager pays the rent. If there is a balance remaining, it is given to the client after the client reviews and signs a monthly statement. Only clients participating in Hope House's Stabilization program are eligible for direct-rent service.

A corollary of HPP is tenant education. As indicated by its name, Hope House's Good Tenant training classes instruct clients in their rights and responsibilities as tenants as well as the rights and responsibilities of the landlord. Upon completion of the training, clients receive certification that is intended to offer a measure of assurance to landlords participating in the program that a client is less risky as a prospective tenant. Through the program, Hope House increases the availability of housing for those who might otherwise be denied it. From Hope House's perspective, clients are building a history of being desirable tenants, not deadbeats.

HPP appeals to the bottom line of landlords. Hope House presents HPP to property owners as a strategy for saving advertisement costs and tenant-search costs as well as other costly aspects of filling rental units. Property owners who work with Hope House have prospective tenants screened and educated by the agency's staff.

Staff Members as Life-Skill Coaches

The director and staff of Stabilization coach clients in other life skills as well. For example, clients often are referred for psychological counseling. The purpose of counseling generally is not so much to treat the individual's pathology as to teach skills for coping with the continual assaults of a poverty-stricken environment.

Initially, many clients react negatively. Whereas you and I might rely on counseling as an acceptable remedy for our private troubles, these clients do not view psychological assistance as therapeutic nor as addressing their immediate needs. As one staff member observed, clients are concerned with survival, not with psychic massaging. To someone who is without food and rent money, psychological counseling seems like a ludicrous solution or no solution. If the case manager believes strongly that counseling is in order, however, he or she contracts with the client to undergo counseling for two or three sessions in exchange for something the client needs, like diapers.

From the standpoint of those who lack money, transportation, and child care, counseling is simply one more place to reach by taking two buses with children in tow. Taking two buses can involve subjecting oneself and one's children to unpleasant weather—rain, snow, sleet, or record high temperatures. Also, the client and the children might be dressed in dirty clothes because there is no money to buy detergent, no laundry facility in the apartment building, and/or no money for the laundromat. Because of her living conditions, it is not unreasonable for a client to resist counseling, which involves telling yet another stranger one's life story.

And what is safe to tell a counselor? For some, who have been in and out of the welfare system for years, counseling represents another form of intrusiveness by numerous strangers, including AFDC workers, food stamp workers, and nonprofit social service agency workers. If one talks about one's anger and rage, could the counselor take the children away? Viewed from a client's perspective, it is easy to understand why a client would choose medication over psychotherapy. By developing a relationship with clients based on advocacy, Stabilization staff members work with clients to allay their fears about counseling as well as many other issues.

SYSTEMIC SOLUTIONS NEEDED

While collaborative programs like Stabilization can and do reduce, by a few, the number of individuals and families who are in poverty and/or lack housing, the impact on poverty overall is negligible. Although programs of this genre have the potential to build on individuals' strengths rather than attack perceived client pathology, individual-based solutions are not enough. Even with a collaborative effort, the resources available are insufficient to serve more than a handful of individuals and families. And Ms. Carrington notes that the individual who arrives at the door of Hope House or any other agency across this nation is perhaps the "strongest" member of the family—the caretaker, the forager, the provider, the most verbal one, the most physically able person, or the one who can read or write. If Stabilization helps, perhaps it is because the case manager interacts with the "cream" of the family—the one selected directly or indirectly by other family members to be the spokesperson. But what about those who do not come for help? If there are not enough resources to go around now, what will happen if more and more people seek assistance, as will be the case when federal monies stop? Should we just write them off? Congress and the president have initiated the dismantling of federal funding for the poor which means that demand will continue to outstrip availability of financial assistance. What are the poor to do? What do we as a society do? What happens to those in poverty eventually affects all of us.

Chapter 6

Consciousness Raising: An Old Solution with a New Twist

Throughout this treatise evidence has been presented to support the claim that due to structural changes in the economy, millions of women and men are unable to play their respective traditional societal roles of nurturer and good provider. Accordingly, the preceding pages have examined the prospects for improvement in the situation of those at the lower end of the socioeconomic scale, and multiple indicators have been cited that suggest a decline. Opportunities for social mobility for this group—structurally distant because of their class position—are more remote now because of the continuing alterations in the economy.

In this chapter a strategy for politicizing the oppressed is revived from the 1970s. Consciousness raising, the alteration of individual fears and anxiety into a collectivity of shared awareness and action, is resurrected and assessed.[1]

What does a society do with those who have become economic cast-offs or with those who were never cast-ons? Do we medicate their emotional depression while ignoring their economic plight? Tranquilizing the economically disenfranchised in order to decrease the probability that millions of people will rise up and rale against the skewed distribution of scarce resources within their midst is draconian, to say the least. Fortunately, there are less extreme solutions to pursue. The question is whether this nation would rather tranquilize or socialize. Policy recommendations for systemic change are spelled out in chapter 7 and the next several pages explore "disalienation" and consciousness raising as strategies for change at the individual level.

DISALIENATION AND CONSCIOUSNESS RAISING

The Concept of Disalienation

Research by David Wagner and Marcia Cohen called for the development of "disalienation" among those who have been deprived of homes, but the concept is useful when discussing the plight of any of those living under poverty conditions. The two researchers defined disalienation as a process by which those in poverty collectively throw off any stigma imposed on them by society. Because their study focused on those without housing, Wagner and Cohen reasoned that perceptions about housing will change only when those without housing demand new thinking about it. It is not a stretch to suggest then that when those in poverty change their self-perceptions, societal views will change.[2]

The reinterpretation offered by Wagner and Cohen summons those at the bottom of the socioeconomic ladder to redefine the alienated image of themselves and their group into a positive collective persona. Those in poverty are challenged to reject their "looking glass self"—the negative self as reflected in the eyes of others.[3] Recall that feeling like the undesirable self, as delineated by Cooley, was a common reaction of women as they used food stamps to buy groceries, carried a Section 8 certificate in search of housing, lived in public housing, and/or lacked a place to live. They poignantly expressed seeing themselves reflected negatively in the eyes of others, of feeling like the other—not accepted, marginal.

Disalienation requires those who feel like the other to reject the negative treatment by those they encounter. For example, all of the women I interviewed spoke of the humiliation they suffered whenever they used their food stamps. The women recounted instances of rude, discourteous store clerks, sneering customers who disapprovingly surveyed the contents of their shopping carts, and even shoppers who gave forceful directives that they get off the dole. The women shook their heads in agreement as each offered her own personal worst experience. One mother told of going to great lengths to shield her daughter from society's negative reflection. Hoping she would be economically independent by the time her daughter was old enough to comprehend AFDC and food stamps, the mother never used food stamps when her daughter accompanied her to the store. The mother expressed fear about the prospects of not realizing the elusive goal of economic independence for her family before her daughter fully understood their economic reality.

Using consciousness raising, a tactic from the 1960s and 1970s, Hope House staff work to create disalienation and redefine reality for the economically disenfranchised women whom they serve.

What Is Consciousness Raising?

Consciousness raising (CR) challenges individuals about what they think and act concerning discrimination and the inequitable conditions of their lives. CR is meant to awaken people to societal conditions that could hinder their full development. It can be a method for guiding the individual's reinterpretation of society's negative reflection of those who are poor, especially women. It is based on the idea that oppression and its resulting self-effacement can be reduced as individuals recognize that their personal situation is tied to the larger political, social, and economic system. Using Mills's sociological imagination, CR empowers individuals to understand how their private troubles are connected to public issues.[4]

Consciousness raising, a strategy initiated by feminists in this country in the 1970s, was directed at heightening women's awareness of their subordinate role in patriarchal society. Appealing to educated middle-class Anglo women, CR helped to mobilize a small proportion of women in birthing the contemporary feminist movement. Ideally, consciousness raising is a forum through which women strategize to reclaim themselves as women, build sisterhood, and in the process reject seeing themselves as objects or property. It is a strategy that encourages women to throw off what Dorothy Smith refers to as their everyday experience in a patriarchal society.[5]

Unlike the women who avail themselves of the services of Hope House because they continually struggle to obtain life's necessities, the women in early CR groups tended to be members of more advantaged socioeconomic status. However, because women living without basic needs routinely expend their intellectual and emotional energy trying to obtain what those in middle and upper classes take for granted, facilitating CR among those in desperate need may be problematic. If CR is to have an impact, hunger and housing requirements may have to be satisfied first. Missionaries have known for centuries the secret of converting indigenous populations: fill their bellies as you fill their minds.

Related to Paulo Freire's work with the peasant class in Brazil and Chile, CR is directed at making the oppressed conscious of the external sources of their misery. Freire's CR follows two dictums: comprehending the destructive aspects of one's social environment and changing the negative elements of the system.[6]

CONSCIOUSNESS RAISING AT HOPE HOUSE

At Hope House I facilitated three consciousness raising sessions and participated in five CR sessions with ten to fifteen shelter guests. About half of the guests came to all the sessions, but because of the turnover in shelter, unfamiliar faces appeared at each gathering. Understandably, every week the new arrivals' anguish about their personal housing problems overshadowed their energy for participating fully in a CR discussion. On the other hand, those who attended all sessions became active and willing participants.

During the ensuing weeks, aspects of racism in the women's

lives (most of the women were African-American), sexism, and the systemic interaction of the "isms" were explored. Each session focused on increasing members' self-awareness, collective cognizance, and subsequent action about each issue.

The "Not Me" Syndrome

Despite obvious socioeconomic differences, the relatively privileged women of the 1970s and the women living in Hope House today have at least one characteristic in common: a lack of consciousness about the existence of systemic sexism and/or racism in their lives. Like young female students in a college classroom, Hope House participants initially expressed individual denial about their experience. Although each member had a vague understanding that racism and sexism existed to some extent in society, according to initial reports, none had experienced any ism individually. They were certain that others with whom they were acquainted had been victimized, but not them.

One by one, the participants recounted discrimination experienced by significant others and tales of discrimination suffered by friends and acquaintances. As if by magic, their initial stories indicated that they had escaped the trauma of racism and sexism endured by those in their midst—mother, father, sister, brother, and other relatives and friends. Even those who said they had attended predominantly Anglo high schools initially claimed feeling untouched by prejudice and discrimination. By their first accounts, they had not been treated as the "other," but had been accepted and included.

The reaction of the women is not uncommon. We tend to accept the dominant ideology and internalize it even when it is not in our interest to do so. Attitudes about society and one's place in society are taken in through the dominant ideology. In the process, one's development is constrained and limited to a certain extent. In consciousness raising, the interactions of the individual and the influence of ideology on that individual are considered.

Denying Racism

As the weeks wore on, the women began to talk of specific incidents and the experience of feeling marginalized and excluded or being treated as objects. Even at that, it was difficult for participants, especially the younger women, to connect their individual experience to systemic racism and/or sexism. One participant, for example, recounted how she had tried to rent an apartment during the preceding week. Even though a sign was posted indicating that an apartment was available, she was told it had been rented. When the sign continued to be posted, she visited a second time, undaunted, and even considered making a third visit to be certain of what she had experienced. When others in the group suggested that she had been discriminated against, it was difficult for her to come to terms with the possibility that she had been subjected to racism. Tearfully, she expressed great distress that people continue to judge others solely on the basis of skin color.

Consciousness Raising and Sexism

Initial reaction to the sessions on sexism were similar to the racism sessions. Staff members' facial expressions betrayed their quiet disbelief as CR participants recounted their tales of "controlling" the men in their lives. The bravado of participants had a surreal quality; young and middle-age women were sitting in a shelter rejecting the concept of sexism in their lives, all the while telling of having suffered abuse and/or witnessing abuse throughout their lives.

Offering examples of their "dominance" over men, each participant attempted to give credence to her status as a liberated woman. One young woman, who claimed that she could get anything she wanted from a man by using sex, enumerated the valuable items she had received from the men in her life. She failed to address her many evictions and shelter stays in a variety of cities, nor the reasons why most of her treasures had disappeared. In recounting her so called sexual domination of men, she failed to take into account what the cost had been for her and her children. When another group member challenged her, asking why she was in a shelter, she fell silent.

Another participant, a teenager who was staying at the shelter with her mother and other siblings, reported that when her fiancé ordered her to perform a domestic chore, his demand sometimes was accompanied with slapping, punching, or kicking. To her way of thinking, his abusive behavior was inconsequential because, as she insisted, she could return the violence punch for punch.

Finally, a middle-aged woman, like a general recounting his successful military campaigns, enumerated her battles in thwarting sexual harassment and rape. Although her trauma occurred both at work and in a personal relationship with a man, she failed to question why she had been subjected to such behavior.

Consciousness Raising and Action for Change

When the women were asked how, as individuals, they could act as agents for change in their own lives to combat the isms, there was agreement among many of the participants on using physical force as a solution. These women, socialized in a concrete world—a world in which survival is the focus of life—and in a society that glamorizes violence have learned concrete methods of coping. Violence, a primordial strategy for releasing anger and rage, was a familiar technique available in their repertoire of behavior. Discussion, compromise, negotiation, and exchange fall within the abstract realm. These strategies require that one have the ability to clearly communicate with another as well as listen to another's version of reality. And an equitable exchange means that the benefits outweigh the cost of the interaction—something those who live in poverty have not come to expect.

What conclusions can we draw about the use of consciousness raising for women without homes? First, as I have noted elsewhere in the text, women who are responsible for their children and who are without homes are trying desperately to attend to, even cling to, a survival mode. Under these circumstances, women will find it difficult, although not impossible, to focus on issues that, while tightly intertwined with their circumstances, seem irrelevant to them at the moment. Be that as it may, by the fourth week the women in the Hope House consciousness raising group began to comprehend the connections between their lives and the larger society, and they plotted collective action, including a group confrontation of the landlord who refused to rent to the African-American woman. They also considered going en masse to an area grocery store that they believed had discriminated against several of the women who had used food stamps in the establishment.

CONSCIOUSNESS RAISING AND WOMEN IN POVERTY

At least for this small sample, we can say that consciousness raising is facilitated as readily as when the participants are middle-class, college-educated women. It is true that women who have been exposed to scholarly teaching and writings about sexism, racism, and classism and have also experienced one or more of these isms in their own lives are equipped to examine issues and solutions conceptually as well as experientially.

On the other hand, women who survive in poverty live a life of discrimination due to isms without time out or a hiatus. One might be inclined to draw the conclusion that a lack of academic knowledge of these issues would be detrimental for their coping skills, but Patricia Hill Collins argues strongly for another interpretation. Although written specifically about the unique experience of African-American women, the following excerpt from Collins is in some ways apropos to Anglo women in poverty as well. According to Collins, there are two ways of knowing, knowledge and wisdom, as she explains:

Living life as black women requires wisdom since knowledge about the dynamics of race, gender, and class subordination has been essential to Black women's survival...The use of experience...has been key to Black women's survival...As members of a subordinate group, Black women cannot afford to be fools of any time, for their devalued status denies them the protections that white skin, maleness, and wealth confer... In the context of race, gender, and class oppression, the distinction is essential since knowledge without wisdom is adequate for the powerful, but wisdom is essential to the survival of the subordinate.[7]

Collins and others maintain that those with formal education do not monopolize all knowledge, only knowledge contained in books. From this perspective, women on the street possess knowledge that is equal in importance to that found in texts.[8] The task for Hope House staff is getting women living in survival circumstances to use their "street smarts" to enhance their lives beyond survival. They view CR as one tool for achieving that. Typically women learn to compete with one another, not cooperate. Women learn to be wary of one another, not trust. Consciousness raising requires that participants let go of preconceived patriarchy-induced ideas and fears about other women, develop trust in one another, and work together for their common good, forming a sisterhood.

Finally, consciousness raising is analogous to Marx's notion of class consciousness. From a Marxian perspective, workers must become aware that they hold economic and political interests in common before any societal change can occur. Like Marx's workers, women, through consciousness raising, are expected to become cognizant of their mutuality, and their group interests and also become aware that their commonalities override their differences. According to Marx, without this step, change will not be forthcoming.

Chapter 7

Recommendations

Some extreme measures could be recommended to redistribute America's wealth. Stephanie Coontz has compiled an impressive list from a variety of sources that include the following:

Redistributing just 1 percent of the income of America's richest 5 percent would lift one million people above the poverty line. A 1 percent tax on the net wealth of the richest 2 percent of American families would allow us to double federal spending on education and still have almost $20 billion left to spend somewhere else. One commission has recently suggested that it would be possible to restructure the military to transfer $125 billion a year to other uses over the next ten years. A mere 1 percent cut in military expenditures would free up enough money to fund the ABC child care bill, double the AIDS research budget, and triple the budget for the homeless. And diverting money from the military to the schools would have other benefits, since $1 billion of spending on missiles creates only 9,000 jobs, and the same amount spent on education creates 63,000 jobs.[1]

It is unlikely that the richest 2 or 5 percent of the population will give up part of their wealth other than through philanthropic measures that provide copious tax deductions for them. It is also improbable that a cut in military spending will be implemented to fund child care. Yet hundreds of thousands of women are forced to forego a job that might keep the family from falling through the cracks or might provide the ticket off of AFDC because safe, affordable child care is not available. Further hundreds of thousands of children are without health insurance; safe, affordable housing; or adequate daily caloric intake. Some of these social issues, debated ad infinitum, could find resolution in a series of social welfare programs.

As I have written these last few pages, a Democratic president, Bill Clinton, has signed a bill to strip away federal support for children and their families who already reside in economic despair. I go forward with my recommendations undaunted by the mood in Washington, understanding that the pendulum will have to swing back because states will falter under the burden that they are being asked to bear. It may occur, as it did the last time, surprisingly, during a Republican administration when then-President Nixon put in place the Food Stamp Program.

Therefore, while the privileged in Washington refuse to hear the cries of the poor, I offer recommendations that would make working beneficial for those receiving AFDC, not costly, as it often is under the current system. Working would make AFDC recipients producers as well as consumers. Many of the ideas discussed here have been suggested elsewhere but bear repeating. Some suggestions are expensive but are fiscally less costly than our current system of dependency, which we who pay for and those who receive disdain but continue to cling to tenaciously. For those on the receiving end, the current system is degrading, decreases their ability to develop fully their gifts and talents, and reduces their potential to be fully contributing members of society. For those who are working and paying taxes, welfare has become America's whipping post.

SOCIAL WELFARE: TOO RADICAL FOR AMERICANS?

People in this country have long opposed government solutions that begin with the word social. The resistance seems to emanate from the almost mythical fear of socialism and communism—the ultimate cold-war, *preglasnost* threat to Western ideology and civilization as people in this country acknowledge it—as well as our religious fervor and belief in pulling oneself up by one's bootstraps. Stephanie Coontz provides an unnerving reminder that few of us are free of some sort of government support, whether it is in the form of student loans, Pell grants, FHA loans, VA loans, social security, Medicare, the GI Bill, unemployment compensation, workers' compensation, farm subsidies, milk subsidies, tobacco subsidies, minimum wage legislation, mortgage and property tax deductions, or medical tax deductions, to name a few.[2]

Although a significant barrier to the acceptance and implementation of social welfare is its socialistic overtone, as Coontz's list of federal assistance indicates, we as a nation are steeped in social welfare. Still another obstacle to national discussion and to the possibility of developing consensus about social welfare is the widespread resistance to paying higher taxes to support programs that are perceived as benefiting selected groups. Acceptance of expanded social programs would more than likely require a protracted struggle similar to the Social Security battle of the 1930s. An epic campaign would have to be forged, championed by a contemporary hero (perhaps a military icon like Colin Powell), to gain citizen support.

Under the umbrella of an American social welfare system, a continuum of food stamps, basic medical insurance, and housing subsidies could be obtained by working-class families. Nationalized day care would be available for all low- and lower middle-income wage earners. In this way sufficient numbers of workers would be guaranteed for the growing number of low-income jobs, and workers would be assured that their basic material needs would be met. Favorable public opinion about universal health care early in the Clinton presidency indicates the support that can be mustered when people are assured they will share in the benefits.

Social welfare programs implemented in western European countries provide models for productive solutions for this nation's welfare "problems." Social programs that have received widespread support and worked well in other countries are those that provide universal coverage so that the fruits of taxation are enjoyed by all.

We Have Been on This Track Too Long

Because employment continues to grow at the low end of the skill and wage scale, most of the traditional, taken-for-granted aspects of work continue to be eroded: full-time hours, fair wages, benefits, and job permanency. The uncertain conditions of the good provider role, as discussed in chapter 3, affect marriage and family formation. In today's market, women and men are reluctant to formalize their relationships, and married couples hesitate to begin families. When those with limited occupational skills find low-end, part-time jobs, they are unlikely to be able to support themselves and their families with their wages. The current job market allows fewer and fewer people to afford a home, start a family, or stabilize a household without receiving some form of assistance. Some scholars, MacDermid and Targ, for example, indicate that there is evidence to suggest that policies affecting families have frequently emanated from the workplace.[3]

In this country a drawback of income-tested welfare as it exists today is that it disallows the working class and members of the middle class to partake of the benefits they subsidize for their fellow citizens at the lower and upper ends of the income scale. Barely managing financially, the working and lower middle classes carry a large proportion of the fiscal burden for all others. If social welfare programs are to gain the support of these two groups, they must enjoy a slice of the pie. Many of the jobs that have been eliminated in recent years were middle management, causing significant downward mobility for this group. Their reversal of fortune economically could make them more responsive to social programs offering universal coverage. On the other hand, those in the working class who spend lives of quiet desperation barely eking out a living, with income too high to qualify for assistance, might be supportive of a social program that included them.

TAX RECOMMENDATIONS

Sweden's Tax Break for Dual Earners

Sweden's separate tax for husbands and wives is one example of a universal coverage program that maximizes a wife's contribution to the family economic unit. In this country, with a progressive tax rate, if a husband and wife file their taxes jointly, a husband's income of $35,000 and his wife's of $22,000 would be taxed at $57,000. Depending on the tax bracket, the wife's income ultimately can financially penalize the family's tax burden.

On the other hand, in Sweden, which does not have a progressive tax structure, assessment of a husband's wages is separate from that of his wife's. The wife's lower income is taxed less. In Sweden, then, the wife's lower income makes a greater contribution to the family's economic well-being than in the United States.[4] Considering just two of Sweden's social welfare programs, a lower tax rate for the member of the household with lower income and national day care, it should come as no surprise that families in Sweden have a higher standard of living than families in this country.

Tax Breaks for the Working Poor

Other forms of social programs designed to alleviate workers' tax burden, especially programs for those who work but whose insufficient earnings keep them in poverty, have been recommended by Eric Lindblom[5] and others. One example is exempting the first several thousand dollars of earnings from social security tax while simultaneously raising the upper amount that can be taxed. Second, raising the Earned Income Credit would bring almost three million families living in poverty (who are headed by someone who works) closer to escaping from poverty. And if food stamp subsidies were retained, these families would benefit further. Lindblom suggests that the $7 billion it would cost to underwrite raising the Earned Income Credit is less costly than raising the minimum wage to $6 an hour (to have the same effect). Still another tax recommendation specifically targeted for those whose earnings fail to lift them out of poverty is the transformation of personal exemptions into refundable tax credit. This strategy would target more of those who are poor than would raising the personal exemption.

Although not an exhaustive list of recommendations for easing the income disparity of those who are poor, this is certainly a doable list if we have the will. The readers' attention is now directed to housing solutions.

HOUSING RECOMMENDATIONS

Volunteerism

As a society, we must face reality. Volunteer organizations cannot replace the diminishing stock of low-income housing needed to meet demand. Certainly Habitat for Humanity and similar organizations are to be commended for their work on behalf of those without housing. Volunteer effort, like most philanthropy, allows people the opportunity to make a contribution to society. Community building, both literal and figurative, makes people feel worthwhile and useful. Civitas—a willingness to help others in the community—is a necessary ingredient in any society, but the effect of volunteerism on the exponential disappearance of the low-income housing stock is illusory. For every building constructed or rehabbed by such groups, perhaps ten buildings in the community (more often than not owned by absentee landlords) are allowed to deteriorate to the point of condemnation when the owners no longer realize a profit. Increasing numbers of families lack homes, and Habitat and other nonprofit groups cannot possibly house all of them. What are we to do?

Subsidized Housing

It has been noted elsewhere in this work that a worker must earn almost $9.00 an hour, working full-time, to pay the rent on a two-bedroom apartment. Millions of workers do not earn $9.00 dollars an hour. Millions earn minimum wage. Therefore, millions of workers clustered at the bottom of the occupational ladder struggle with the barest of necessities—housing. It means that millions of employees who show up for work every day are able to afford housing only if they live in some form of subsidized, public, or shared housing. In New York, 150,000 families are waiting for Section 8 vouchers. In Los Angeles, the waiting list has 40,000, and no new applications can be taken until 2001.[6] As a society, the sooner we acknowledge housing as an issue, the sooner the problem can be ameliorated.

For the many who are working part-time at minimum wage, housing assistance will need to be in place indefinitely. At that low level of income, few families will become solvent in one year or even five. Subsidized housing must be viewed as a long-term solution. No reduction in transfer payments should occur unless the amount received makes an individual's or a family's income equal to 150 percent the fair-market rent in the area where they live.[7] Because of the persistence of current job market conditions, this recommendation is not unreasonable. Families with members working full-time but whose wages are at the low end of the income scale will continue to need support for basic necessities. Public assistance for low-end workers will disappear only as earnings increase.

The severe shortage of affordable housing calls for drastic measures and creative thinking. Solutions might even be found in a return to discarded ways of doing things. Just as today's medical community has reinstated the medieval practice of using leeches for certain health problems, so too our local and federal policy makers might do well to reconsider some of the practices of housing and assisting families that have been cast aside.

Expanding Section 8 Housing

One housing program that Congress has been cutting into and has longed to rescind completely is Section 8 housing. Yet for decades it has been an important form of permanent housing for low-income people. Currently Section 8 helps 3.6 million people obtain housing, but landlords have been doing a mass exodus from Section 8 because the subsidy they receive from the government has been decreasing.[8] Fewer landlords participating in the program means fewer units exist to house low-income families. It is instructive that Section 8 was initiated during the Nixon era and is being dismantled under President Clinton. So much for the conservative-liberal argument.

In the face of the cutbacks, suggesting that the program be expanded is anathema to the Republicans, with their current "slash and burn" view of social welfare. But that is what is being proposed here, as others have proposed elsewhere.[9] Under the current program, individuals living alone or unrelated persons living together cannot avail themselves of Section 8 benefits. Including these groups in the program increases the price tag roughly between $8 and $12 billion dollars. It sounds costly, but it addresses the issue of prevention-intervention, and stabilizes individuals and families. The cost could be reduced if Section 8 housing regulations were written so that the cap on that portion of income to be set aside for rent were pushed above the current figure of 30 percent. Some may wince at this suggestion, thinking it fiscally unwise to require people to pay more than 30 percent of their income for housing, but regulating rents to 35 to 40 percent of a family's income would realize a savings for the program. Although ideally everyone would like to pay a third of their income for housing, most pay more. The bottom line is that when people are able to resolve their housing, health needs, child care, and food needs in an affordable manner, they can accept a minimum-wage job. Expanding Section 8 is one option; it is not the only option.

Shared Housing

Over time, as the standard of living has increased in the United States, we have rejected the idea of sharing space, whether in a home or a room. In ideal circumstances, every child has his or her own room, Dad has his special area, and Mom has a space of her own. New houses boast a living room, a family room, rooms for study, exercise, and entertainment, even a "great room." Spaciousness attests to our affluence. It is instructive that in our society as family size continues to shrink, the square footage of new houses expands. Consequently, at the upper-income levels of society, a few are living in more space. However, at the lower-income levels, less living space is available, and increasing numbers of people have no space at all. Short of confiscating upper-income people's homes to convert them to communal living quarters, what can we do as a society?

Some solutions require an attitude adjustment, not money, but a change in thinking can be as difficult to come by as money. Why not share housing? It has been a mainstay of every society, including this one. Encouraging, permitting, and enabling families to take into their home others who are in crisis is a simple, inexpensive, humanistic solution for housing—public or private.

In my own childhood, an aunt and uncle took my family (including me, my mother, my two sisters, and our dog) into their small house for several months at a time whenever my family was without a home. The four of us slept on one mattress on the floor in the unfinished attic. We shared not only their home but also the use of their water, heat, telephone, and washer, as well as some of their food. Had our dreadful circumstances occurred today, and had my aunt and uncle lived in public housing, we could have risked ejection by the housing authority if our presence had become known. Worse yet, our presence would have jeopardized my uncle and aunt's housing.

Unfortunately, today many families could not share space with their kin or friends even temporarily because of stringent rules in public housing that forbid the practice or because of lease restrictions. It is estimated that keeping a family out of shelter saves $675 to $3,750 a month, depending on the size of the family and the cost of living in the region. As federal funding disappears and demand outstrips supply, communities will become desperate to place families. Shared housing is an idea whose time has come—again.

Bold housing strategies provide families with incentives, not disincentives, to double up in one house or one apartment. Creative housing entails relaxing the rules about family size in public housing and not placing the host's food stamps or transfer payments in jeopardy because someone else is staying on the premises. Currently, federal regulations forbid these practices. It is an example of the imposition of a middle-class standard of living and values on a population whose lives of poverty reflect a nomadic existence. Using Skolnick's analogy, as I did earlier in the text, the living conditions of millions of people subsisting in our midst reflect a preindustrial or early industrial standard of living. Yet as a society, we insist on imposing a postindustrial standard on their lives. It will not work. Facilitating and encouraging families to pool their resources as people did in earlier eras might be their only hope for survival.

Stabilizing families implies correcting a course that is careening in a downward spiral to the eventual loss of permanent housing. Realistically, stabilizing families does not mean providing the extras of middle-class comfort; it means empowering families and individuals to meet minimum physical needs of housing and food. Stabilization must precede attempts to start individuals on the path toward self-sufficiency.

Boarding Houses

Without moving a brick, without picking up a hammer, those lacking homes could be housed today, but it would require altering our thinking about home as our private haven and changing our local housing ordinances. Existing private homes could house a significant number of those without homes. Close to 5 million homes with multiple bedrooms in this country have one person living in them.[10] Zoning codes and laws would have to be reversed or altered to permit the use of single-family homes as multiple-family dwellings—boarding houses—in residential areas. Tax credits could be offered as an incentive for people to share their homes.

One group that could benefit from shared housing is the elderly. A growing population, the elderly would gain economically and emotionally from the arrangement. It would give the elderly (especially women, who are more likely to be alone and have an increased probability of being poor) added income. And it would provide a return to some semblance of family living, providing an escape from loneliness for elderly widows and/or widowers, especially those without families or friends in close proximity to care for them.

Although housing represents a primary concern for achieving independence as well as a major chunk of an individual's paycheck, it is not the only issue for many who are trying to survive. Another problem that has to be addressed when discussing work and family concerns is child care.

WORKING POOR: AN OXYMORON

Jobs That People Cannot Afford to Fill

As noted in chapter 2, full-time employment at $5.15 an hour is necessary to replace what a mother receives for her children in transfer payments. When a mother forfeits AFDC and obtains a job, she must earn more than $5.15 an hour to pay the additional expenses she will incur when leaving AFDC. Her earnings have to compensate for the loss of food stamps, medical care, and rent assistance. Also, a job brings new expenses, like child care, clothing, and transportation, in addition to the basic monthly costs of shelter and food. An hourly wage of $5.15 cannot be stretched to meet all of the needs listed.

Hundreds of thousands of part-time, low-paying, no-benefit, dead-end jobs are available, and more are created every day. Despite the unattractiveness of these jobs, there are hundreds of thousands of poor people who are willing to take those jobs. Many have tried and have had to fall back on AFDC, as they soon find that they cannot support a family on part-time wages. It is instructive that 40 percent of poor persons aged 15 and older work, and 25 percent of workers who are poor are employed full-time. The last statistic is an unpleasant reminder that a 40-hour-a-week job is not always the solution for escaping poverty.[11] How do we reconcile the discrepancy between the needs of the workplace and the needs of potential workers?

A Family Wage for Women

One recommendation long overdue is a family wage for women. The most important mechanism for lifting working women out of poverty is for employers to pay women wages that are equivalent to men's wages. For too long women's wages have reflected the era of the "living wage"—a time when a woman's wage was meant only to sustain her minimally. Women's wages today are reminiscent of a time when the bulk of a woman's support was supposed to come from a woman's father, brother, uncle, or other male kin.[12] A woman's wage was intended to keep her from becoming attached to the workplace, an arena viewed as unsavory and too vulgar for a woman's moral character.

Even with that, consider that a woman working full-time at minimum wage in the 1960s and 1970s (two decades in which the term female head of household was an anomaly) could keep a family of three out of poverty. Today a woman working under those circumstances has an annual deficit of $2,300. Although working full-time is a necessity, a family cannot survive on minimum wage for full-time work.[13] The issue of women's pay equity becomes even more salient in the face of male household heads' diminishing ability to support families.

FAMILY: AN INCLUSIVE DEFINITION

Family as a Social Construct

Today there are some family scholars who might argue that paying women a family wage would further undermine the two-parent structure. But still others contend that family is a social construct—and as such is defined by the social group.[14] From this perspective then, the two-parent nuclear family is not necessarily an inherent characteristic of the family institution, but is time and culture bound. Defining family structure within this framework, its fluidity and dynamic quality can be appreciated. The family is not a static entity. With that in mind, then, the single-parent family, the recombined family, the biological two-parent family, as well as other family forms all can be acknowledged as valid family forms. Further, if one accepts the notion of diversity of family, then a family wage cannot be denied women, especially those who are single heads of household. Discrimination in the workplace on the basis of gender (or race) has been outlawed for more than two decades, yet wage discrimination continues to account for about half of the wage gap between women and men. Paying women wages equitable to mens' would go a long way in pulling women and children out of poverty.

Paying female employees wages equitable to men's fits with a new ideology of the family. It veers from the concept of father as sole support. It dismisses the notion of deadbeat dad. Paying women a wage equitable to men's writes a new script for families that redefines marital partnership and is reminiscent of other time periods when women contributed as much as men to the economic well-being of the family. There are many other measures that can be considered to address the issue of poverty for families, but not without a struggle. For example, as states push mothers with small children into the workplace, child care will be pushed to the forefront of this nation's political agenda.

Child Care: National or Subsidized

Lack of safe, affordable child care prevents many working-class, lower middle-class, middle-class, and especially poor women from taking jobs. How will this nation's fragmented, individualistic child care function when millions of new workers search for safe, affordable child care for their children? Today 46 percent of all child care is provided by parents and about 15 percent by other relatives. The remainder is provided at child-care centers and at home-centered nonrelative sites (21 percent and 3 percent respectively). Women earning minimum wage or even $5.00 an hour cannot afford child care. Although the costs vary widely by region (from $3,100 in Florida to $7,200 in Boston), a female single head of household earning minimum wage could not pay for child care in either place.[15]

In a government study of child care in seven states, researchers found that five states have inadequate funding for child care for families who receive AFDC and have members who want either to work or to participate in job training. States have been threatening to enact tougher standards for financial assistance. For example, although Michigan has a shortage of child-care providers (especially for families who are poor), lawmakers proposed that mothers go to work 12 weeks after the birth of a child.[16] If middle-income and upper-income women are unable to resolve the child-care problem easily and permanently, how are the poor to do so? Is the care of poor children less important?

Tax credits are appropriate for child care in middle- and upper-income families, but not for lower-income workers. The latter group has a cash flow problem and cannot wait for an income tax refund to pay for child care. They need money now. Unfortunately, tax credits are a form of savings legislated by a body of privileged persons who generally lack firsthand knowledge about the hand-to-mouth existence of many Americans—or even about the cost of a gallon of milk.

Other options would be more useful for families. For example, child-care vouchers for low-income families would be a benefit because vouchers provide payment when the service is utilized. Nationalized child care would be more effective because it would serve all children whose parents work and need the service. More than 50 percent of mothers with small children are in the work force, but fewer than 20 percent of children receive care in a child-care center. The vast majority of families must arrange for child care without assistance from their employer or their government. As noted, typically families make piecemeal arrangements using a variety of sources including spouses, grandparents, other relatives, neighbors, and friends. While there is a constant hue and cry about the slothfulness of women receiving AFDC, few solutions have been forthcoming to address the issue of child care. A government study of availability of child care in seven states found that five states (Idaho, Maryland, Montana, North Dakota, and South Carolina) were unable to accommodate the child-care needs of families receiving AFDC. Therefore, people wanting to take a job were unable to do so.[17] In one county in Ohio, $11 million was spent last year on child care so that women receiving AFDC could get a job. What will happen to those families when the federal government withdraws its funding? Do you think that mothers with low-wage potential can pick up the cost of their child care? Do you think that the states will be able to pick up the slack?

The United States and South Africa are the only two industrialized nations that have resisted establishing nationalized day care. South Africa (under the regime of Nelson Mandela) is likely to implement it before the United States does. With the proportion of dual-earner families increasing, nationalized child care is long overdue. However, as long as child care is viewed as a women's issue or a mothers' issue rather than a family issue, the burden will continue to fall on women to find solutions at the individual level. When fathers in the legislature and fathers in corporations join forces with the millions of women who have been calling for child-care assistance, solutions will be forthcoming. And when employers want to replace high-priced male workers with less costly female employees, they will give attention to this issue.

SUBSIDIES

Food Stamp and Other Subsidies

At the present time, individuals and families can receive food stamps if their income does not increase by a specified amount, depending on the size of the family. For families whose wages are not likely to rise much beyond the minimum during their working lives because of their low skill level and/or the uncertainties of the job market, there is little incentive to work. The benefit of working at minimum wage, after adjusting for inflation, is at its lowest since the late 1960s. Simply put, the costs of going to work are greater than the rewards. Low-wage workers stand to lose more than they gain from employment. Employment carries additional costs, including child care, clothing, transportation, and medical care, and it is not possible for families to absorb these costs if they earn minimum wage. We as a society need to face the reality. Households whose workers' wages hover around the minimum will require continued housing assistance, food stamp allotment, child care, and medical care if they are to work and survive.

Nonfood Stamp Subsidies and Public Health

In addition to continuing food stamp subsidies, the implementation of nonfood stamp subsidies deserves serious consideration. Some of the most expensive items in a household's grocery shopping cart are nonfood products such as bath soap, dish detergent, clothing detergent, cleanser, bleach, toilet paper, disposable diapers, facial tissue, paper towels, and toothpaste. Because a family's food stamp allotment can be used for food items only, most families and individuals in poverty go without the ingredients necessary for instilling habits of cleanliness in children.

Consider the problems faced by a parent who wants to teach her child hygienic habits but lacks the tools. Is she supposed to tell the child, "If we had soap, this is how we would wash our hands?" Children learn by imitation; if the child sees her parents using soap, she will do likewise. If the behavior is not modeled for the child, the likelihood of learning the behavior decreases. Personal hygiene might seem to be a private matter, but communicable diseases are a public health concern. If children do not learn personal hygiene at home, they are less likely to adopt hygienic habits when they work in a restaurant or other food service establishment (no matter how many signs employers post telling employees to wash their hands), and that concerns all of us.

THE TRANSITION TO INDEPENDENCE

Beyond Shelter, Beyond Stabilizing Families

Throughout this book, temporary shelters have been cited as the imperfect solution but the best our society has to offer. At the same time, strategies that promote intervention and prevention have been touted as critical for stabilizing families. One model program is worth reviewing. It has the transitional components that President Clinton championed four years ago but has now abandoned. The program offers families a second chance, or a chance to play catch-up. Jocelyn Carrington, executive director of Hope House, described a housing project that the agency has developed. The project, though small in scope, includes temporary housing, an intergenerational facility that will serve as a senior-citizen center, a community center for residents, and a child-care facility. A family can remain in an apartment for up to 6 years, on condition that the head of household makes steady progress toward obtaining a diploma, a degree, or training for an above-minimum-wage occupation, especially occupations that have the potential to bring higher wages, like plumbing or carpentry. Participants in the program will have housing, food stamps, medical care, and child care in place while the heads of household pursue a self-regimented path to economic independence. In one sense the program gives heads of household a hiatus from the ravages and insecurity of poverty by covering a family's basic needs. Once material conditions are stabilized, the head of household can concentrate on acquiring marketplace skills that lead to economic independence.

As the buildings that house Hope House's transitional housing program are renovated and the intergenerational facility is designed and constructed, Ms. Carrington speaks adamantly about what she regards as a crucial component of the program: collaboration with the business community as well as the community as a whole. She explains that individuals enrolled in the program require many forms of support, including child-care assistance, educational and career mentoring, networks, internships, (of course) employment, and, especially, emotional support (from peers enrolled in the program, case managers, and, she hopes, from outside mentors). Most important, those enrolled will need an employer willing to pay a wage that allows them to be self-sustaining. Partnership with community businesses is crucial to the economic independence of program participants.

According to Carrington's estimation, beyond graduation, program participants more than likely will require continued mentoring and monitoring. At the professional level, they will need assistance with resume writing and interviewing strategies. Peer support groups and professional mentors will be invaluable as the participants cope with their life in transition. Socially, they may feel as though they fit comfortably in neither their new environment nor the old, and they may require guidance in successfully bridging the two worlds. Participants' relationships and coping skills will be honed so that they can assuage family members who may feel threatened by participants' achievements and new status as the participants' opportunities broaden and their family and friendship relationships change.

CONCLUSION

Although generally not widely articulated, social class and class mobility can be paired with religion and politics as taboo subject matter for conversations. The omission of class as a polite topic has to do, in part, with a collective failure to admit the relative impermeability of class boundaries in our society. Yet social mobility research consistently demonstrates the lack of significant, dramatic movement of groups within the class structure. Most changes in class position occur incrementally. That being the case, we can expect that perhaps a third of those living in poverty will, at best, become working-class in their lifetime.

What about the other two-thirds? The recommendations delineated here clearly come down on the side of national programs and policies designed to augment the anemic impact of minimum wage and near-minimum wages for individuals and families.

Solutions must emphasize the safety, security, and nurturance of children to prevent the repetition of poverty in the next generation. Today, interventions occur only after a family's home is lost. Tomorrow, policy considerations would do well to adhere to a fundamental point: The most cost-effective solution for issues surrounding the lack of permanent housing is preventing any child and any parent from experiencing the social and economic costs of being without a home.

Epilogue

Connecting Private Troubles with Public Issues: A Little Sociological Imagination Would Help

C. Wright Mills, in discussing the "sociological imagination," entreated us to develop the ability to connect our private troubles with public issues—to recognize that what happens to us as individuals is related to the structure of society.[1] People blame themselves for many of their negative experiences: divorce, out-of-wedlock childbirth, unemployment, poverty, rape, robbery, and being without a home. From Mills's perspective, for societal change to occur, it is essential for people to understand that their troubles are linked with those of others.

The private-public connection enables people to comprehend their anguish about an individual "failed" performance. In fact, Mills would argue, a significant proportion of the blame for what happens to individuals can be shifted to the social system. For example, as has been argued through out this work, it is the system that has failed to provide adequately paying jobs so that people can obtain decent, affordable housing. Further, the declining stock of low-income housing has systemic roots. Understanding the structural constraints impinging on individual action can assuage an individual's feelings of failure and act as a catalyst for societal change to occur.

Age of first marriage is an example of a link between private troubles and public issues. The age of both women and men for first-time marriage has been climbing. Failure to distinguish between micro- and macro-level linkages typically leads to conclusions about the issue that focus on a lack of moral values among young people, with premarital sex and out-of-wedlock births frequently cited as evidence.

On the other hand, a person with Mills's sociological imagination would understand that marriage reflects systemic issues that corrolate with individual behavior. In economically healthy times, for example—marked by a low unemployment rate, rising income, job security, and low inflation—people tend not to delay first marriage. In times of economic reversal, however, people delay formalizing their unions. In chapter 3 evidence was offered indicating that marriage is less likely to occur when the traditional provider cannot obtain steady employment. Further, it was noted that an increasing proportion of women and men (especially African-American men) are losing the ability to fulfill the good-provider role. Delayed marriage and increased out-of-wedlock childbirth then are correlated with the material condition in which people find themselves today.

According to Mills's view, assumptions on the part of political and spiritual leaders about the moral bankruptcy of poor couples who have children outside marriage represents a failure to connect the macro level with the micro. To link macro with micro variables, factors extraneous to the individual are important to consider, such as birth rates in different segments of the population, the relationship between unemployment rates and out-of-wedlock birth rates, and the relationship between out-of-wedlock birth rates and average age at onset of menses. Mills would argue that we must attend to events in the individual's environment that affect his or her behavior. We need to look beyond the obvious to understand an individual's plight.

Following up on the issue of declining values, especially among the poor, I offer a final illustration of our failure to connect the private with the public by examining the relationship among several variables—later age at first marriage, males' inability to fulfill the good-provider role, and younger average age at onset of menses. Rather than considering the interaction of these societal influences on individuals' decisions, fingers are pointed at the supposed immorality and promiscuity of those who conceive outside marriage. Broad generalizations are made comparing today's family values with those of other periods.[2] However, conception outside marriage is not a twentieth-century phenomenon; it has been prevalent in other eras. Yet other time periods are cited today as paragons of unparalleled moral superiority. For example, the eighteenth and nineteenth centuries are deemed to be virtuous epochs when sexuality was beyond reproach and out-of-wedlock births were less common. Often, young women of those times married before they were able to conceive (only about 13 percent of females were fecund by age 18).[3] Early teen pregnancy was less likely to occur then and the probability of conception occurring outside marriage would have been lower.

Today the sequence of marriage and of fecundity has been reversed. Because of a higher standard of living and better nutrition, menses tends to begin in preteen or early teen years. Marriage, on the other hand, is occurring later, largely because of the economic uncertainty for young couples. From Mills's perspective, conception is less likely to be followed by marriage today because young males are increasingly unable to support a family, and couples are less likely to formalize a union without a degree of economic stability.

Mills would call attention to the systemic conditions to which young people are subjected. We live in a society in which premarital and extramarital sexual behavior are embedded within our popular culture, especially in films, music, and television. It is unrealistic to think that young people will remain unaffected by what is modeled for them in entertainment form and in the sexual escapades of politicians and celebrities flaunted and glamorized, even rewarded by enhanced fame and fortune. Further, it is unreasonable to continue adhering to a double standard of sexuality that expects women, but not men, to be immune to the explicit and implicit sexual messages that permeate our culture.[4] In short, a perspective reminiscent of Mills's would argue for a need to look beyond the individual in order to more fully understand his or her behavior.

Although a society's conception of morality plays a role in mating behavior, the process is governed in large part by economics. As argued above, couples tend to delay marriage and the start of a family during economically troubled periods. They do so not because of a lack of family values but because of the material conditions in which they find themselves. Individuals and couples defer major life decisions until they attain financial stability, a process that is taking longer for more and more couples.

The issues facing women, men, and their children who live in poverty and/or who lack a home are multiple, complex, and systemic. The pursuit and implementation of problem-solving strategies, hindered by the words and deeds of politicians, journalists, and evangelists, do little more than focus on deriding those who are poor. Too often their rhetoric implies moral degeneracy on the part of those living in poverty, especially those who receive governmental assistance.

Unfortunately, divisive speeches give permission for constituents to displace their dissatisfaction with their leaders with anger toward the more vulnerable in society. Simply put, encouraging people to blame the victims, not the politicians, is an effective tool. Such encouragement reinforces the resentment felt by working people when they see their tax dollars underwriting income transfer programs to which they have no access, programs that exist for people whom they believe are undeserving.

We, as a society, are challenged to do more than look to not-for-profit service providers in our midst, because while the credo of social work espouses systemic change, in practice social work supports the status quo. Traditional service providers typically tape together the hemorrhaging wounds of individuals' lives and send each person back, scars unformed, to face an unhealed world. It is no more effective than sending the "clean" junkie back to his old neighborhood or the paroled thief back to his consorts in crime. Just as the environment has to be changed for the latter two if they are to start anew, so too must it be changed for those in poverty. A bag of groceries and utility assistance does not alter the dearth of decent-paying jobs or the unavailability of safe, low-income housing. There has to be structural change.

While federal, state, and local funding for bandaid solutions continue to dry up, those living in poverty are bleeding to death. Treating the symptoms of the individual without attacking systemic causes is fiscally futile and, more important gives cruel and false hope to those who are living on the edge of economic and emotional despair. Table E.1 illustrates the poverty rate of this country vis-à-vis other Western democracies. Is our standing in child poverty the way we wish to be remembered as a nation? We must do more.

Table E.1

Child Poverty Rates in Selected Industrialized Countries

Country	Rate
United States (1991)	21.5
Canada (1991)	12.5
Italy (1991)	9.6
Norway (1991)	4.6
Belgium (1992)	3.8
Denmark (1992)	3.3
Sweden (1992)	2.7
Norway (1991)	2.5

Source: The State of America's Children Yearbook 1996 (Washington, D.C.: Children's Defense Fund), p. 6.

As I conclude this treatise, welfare as we know it today costs $25 billion dollars a year. It represents a mere 9 percent of this nation's defense budget and a meager 14 percent of what Medicare costs.[5] And yet welfare as we know it is ending. A new era is emerging for children who are poor, and it is not a kinder, gentler era. It represents a new form of societal violence against the most vulnerable among us. What is instructive about the new era is that a Democratic president is paving its way.

Like the descent to poverty, typically a long, torturous downward spiral, and like tremors that forewarn a major earthquake, the era of welfare reform has been fomenting for some time. In 1992, Bill Clinton promised that he would change welfare as we know it, but he told the nation a transition period was necessary to allow those in poverty to obtain training on their way to economic independence.[6] Clinton argued that it would cost about $10 billion dollars to accomplish this goal. The president's words might have registered 1 on the welfare-reform seismograph. Welfare-reform speeches seem to come every four years.

However, a tremor that would have measured about 3 on the welfare-reform seismograph occurred in 1995 with the Republicans' contract with America. The austere, perhaps even mean-spirited, plan was made worse by Newt Gingrich's inflammatory comments about the lack of family values, especially among those receiving AFDC. In short, Gingrich "put out a contract" on welfare and in the process earned the nickname Grinch or Scrooge.

In 1996, a presidential election year, Bill Clinton, a Democratic president, set off a major earthquake—an 8 on the Richter scale. His signature on the welfare legislation will cut $56 billion from federal assistance for women and children in poverty over the next five years, including the food stamp program (a program initiated during the Nixon presidency).

No federal substitute will replace AFDC and food stamps, and there are no state guarantees for those in poverty. Each state will decide how and whether to assist residents who are living in poverty. But how can states do better than the federal government with

$56 billion dollars less to distribute? Even before the proposed cuts take effect, cities have been unable to care for those who are poor. New York is a prime example. Seventy percent of New York State's recipients of government assistance live in New York City. In fact, New York City has more people receiving assistance than most states.[7]

There are other large cities facing similar problems. For example, Philadelphia's budget for housing for those without homes (even before proposed federal cutbacks) has been exceeded by $4 million. Housing advocates warn that a bad situation will get worse, noting that ten programs that assist in housing the poor have been cut in the last year. Troubling as that is, city services already buckling under the weight of increased demand will be further strained in the wake of federal and state cuts. One issue facing city officials in Philadelphia is the economic and social fallout they will face from a proposed state measure that will end benefits for indigent single men, 18,000 of whom live in Philadelphia.[8]

What will happen in 5 years as the desperation of the poor is exacerbated? An increase in violent crime, including mugging, robbery, burglary, and murder could result.

One of the fallacies surrounding the push to legislate the federal cuts is that only those without jobs are poor. The fact that at least 30 million people work full-time, year round, and are so poor they cannot afford life's basic necessities (as has been discussed throughout this work) is ignored by politicians and pundits alike. The situation of many living in Harlem is instructive. In Harlem, 67 percent of households have at least one member working full-time, yet 40 percent are living in poverty. And while politicians insinuate that there are jobs going begging, the ratio of job seekers to job holders in Harlem is 14 to 1.[9]

If those who are poor are maligned and misjudged, consider the schizophrenic treatment of women by our leaders in the Congress, in the White House, and in the pulpit. On the one hand, there is a nostalgia for a return of fathers as heads of household and mothers as stay-at-home moms. Some argue for a return to a family wage so that women and children can be economically supported by men.[10] On the other hand, the end to welfare as we know it means that without federal assistance, millions of women will be forced to leave their children and head for the workplace. Why is it that mothers and fathers who are poor are viewed differently than are parents in other classes? Why is it that the relationship that parents who are poor have with their children seems to be perceived by our society as less sacrosanct, less endangered by disruption, than that of parents in other classes?

Notes

INTRODUCTION

1. Stephanie Golden, *The Women Outside: Meanings and Myths of Homelessness* (Berkeley: University of California Press, 1992), 100–10.

CHAPTER 1

1. Eric Lindblom, "Toward a Comprehensive Homelessness-Prevention Strategy," *Housing Policy Debate* 2 (1991): 961.

2. Ibid., 29.

3. Ibid.

4. Erving Goffman, *Stigma: Notes on the Management of Spoiled Identity* (Englewood Cliffs, N.J.: Prentice Hall, 1963).

5. Ibid., 5.

6. Eric Lindblom, "Toward a Comprehensive," 961; Peter H. Rossi, *Down and Out in America: The Origins of Homelessness* (Chicago: University of Chicago Press, 1989), 145–55.

7. Martha Burt, *Over the Edge: The Growth of Homelessness in the 1980s* (New York: Russell Sage Foundation, 1992), 21.

8. Alice S. Baum and Donald W. Burnes, *A Nation in Denial: The Truth about Homelessness* (Boulder: Westview Press, 1993), 163–66; Burt, *Over the Edge*, 121.

9. Burt, *Over the Edge*, 122.

10. Erving Goffman, *Asylum* (Garden City, N.Y.: Anchor Books, 1961).

11. Marta Elliot and Lauren J. Krivo, "Structural Determinants of Homelessness in the United States," *Social Problems* 38 (1991): 126.

12. Leona L. Bachrach, "Homeless Women: A Context for Health Planning," *The Milbank Quarterly* 65 (1987): 371–96.

13. David R. Dupper and Anthony P. Halter, "Barriers in Educating Children from Homeless Shelters: Perspectives of School and Shelter Staff," *Social Work in Education* 16 (1994): 39.

14. Michelle Fryt Lineham, "Children Who Are Homeless: Educational Strategies for School Personnel," *Phi Delta Kappan* (September 1992): 62.

15. Doug A. Timmer, D. Stanley Eitzen, and Kathryn D. Talley, *Paths to Homelessness: Extreme Poverty and the Urban Housing Crisis* (Boulder: Westview Press, 1994), 73–74.

16. Crystal Mills and Hiro Ota, "Homeless Women with Minor Children in the Detroit Metropolitan Area," *Social Work* (November 1989): 485.

17. Kathleen Mullan Harris, "Life after Welfare: Women, Work, and Repeat Dependency," *American Sociological Review* 61 (June 1996): 24.

18. Burt, *Over the Edge,* 33; Mary E. Stefl, "The New Homeless: A National Perspective," in *Homeless in Contemporary Society*, edited by Richard D. Bingham, Roy E. Green, and Sammis B. White (Newbury Park, Calif.: Sage, 1987), 46–63.

19. Jonathan Kozol, *Rachel and Her Children: Homeless Families in America* (New York: Fawcett Columbine, 1988).

20. Timmer, Eitzen, and Talley, *Paths*, 93.

21. Rossi, *Down and Out in America*, 181.

22. Elliott and Krivo, "Structural Determinants," 115.

23. Kathy Miller, "Work, Family, and the Good Provider Role: Factors Affecting Rural and Farm Women's Work in Indiana from 1900–1958," (paper presented at the North Central Sociological Association Conference, Cincinnati, Ohio, April 13, 1996).

24. Lynn Y. Weiner, *From Working Girl to Working Mother: The Female Labor Force in the United States, 1820–1980* (Chapel Hill: University of North Carolina Press, 1985), 52.

25. Chester Hartman, *Yerba Buena: Land Grab and Community Resistance in San Francisco* (San Francisco: Glide Publications, 1974), 97.

26. Stanley Eitzen and Maxine Baca Zinn, *In Conflict and Order: Understanding Society* (Boston: Allyn and Bacon, 1993), p 451.

27. Elliott and Krivo, "Structural Determinants," 115.

28. Ibid., 124.

29. C. Wright Mills, *The Sociological Imagination* (New York: Oxford University Press, 1959).

30. Burt, *Over the Edge*, 45.

31. Timmer, Eitzen, Talley, *Paths,* 92.

32. Ibid., 93.

CHAPTER 2

1. George Ellington, *The Women of New York* (New York: New York Book, 1869), 640.

2. Weiner, *From Working Girl*, 63.

3. David Popenoe, "American Family Decline, 1960–1990: A Review and Appraisal," *Journal of Marriage and the Family* 55 (1993): 527–42; Judith Stacey, "The New Family Values Crusaders," *The Nation*, July 25/August 1, 1994, 122.

4. Stephanie Golden, *The Women Outside: Meanings and Myths of Homelessness* (Berkeley: University of California Press, 1992), 121.

5. David Blankenhorn, "Does Grandmother Know Best?" *Family Affairs* 3 (1990): 13–16.

6. Coontz, *The Way,* 262.

7. Peter L. Berger and Thomas Luckmann, *The Social Construction of Reality* (New York: Doubleday, 1966).

8. *The State of America's Children 1992,* (Washington, D.C.: Children's Defense Fund), 31.

9. *The State of America's Children Yearbook 1996* (Washington, D.C.: Children's Defense Fund), 7.

10. Timmer, Eitzen, and Talley, *Paths,* 60, 134, 138.

11. *The State of America's Children Yearbook 1996,* 7.

12. Timmer, Eitzen, and Talley, *Paths,* 173-175.

13. Mills and Ota, "Homeless Women," 485.

14. Timmer, Eitzen, and Talley, *Paths*, 74.

15. Shelley M. MacDermid and Dena B. Targ, "A Call for Greater Attention to the Role of Employers in Developing, Transforming, and Implementing Family Policies," *Journal of Family and Economic Studies* 16 (1995): 155.

16. *The State of America's Children Yearbook 1996,* 3.

17. Coontz, *The Way*, 262.

18. Greg J. Duncan and Willard Rodgers, "Has Children's Poverty Become More Persistent?" *American Sociological Review* 56 (1991): 548.

19. Robert D. Hershey, Jr. "Thesis: Wage Rise Will Hurt Teenagers," *New York Times*, July 9, 1996, C 6.

20. Robert B. Reich, *The Work of Nations* (New York: Vintage, 1991), 204–05.

21. Simon Head, "The New, Ruthless Economy," *The New York Review of Books*, February 26, 1996, 48.

22. "The Flap Over Executive Pay," *Business Week,* May 6, 1991, 91. reprinted in *Sociology: Windows on Society*, edited by John W. Heeren and Marylee Mason (Los Angeles: Roxbury, 1994): 89–94.

23. Thomas A. Moore, *The Disposable Work Force: Worker Displacement and Employment Instability in America* (Hawthorne, N.Y.: Aldine Deupree Gruyter, 1996), 83.

24. Coontz, *The Way*, 273.

25. Head, "The New," 48.

26. Popenoe, "American Family," 528–30.

27. Arlie Hochschild, *The Second Shift* (New York: Viking, 1989).

28. Coontz, *The Way,* 259.

29. Popenoe, "American Family," 531.

30. Judith Stacey, "Backward toward the Postmodern Family: Reflections on Gender, Kinship, and Class in the Silicon Valley," in *Rethinking the Family: Some Feminist Questions*, edited by Barrie Thorne and Marilyn Yalom (Boston: Northeastern University Press, 1992), 101.

31. Coontz, *The Way*, 265.

32. Timmer, Eitzen, and Talley, *The Path.*

33. Robert D. Hershey, Jr., "U.S. Jobless Rate for June at 5.3%: Lowest in 6 Years," *New York Times*, July 6, 1996, front page.

34. MacDermid and Targ, "A Call For," 154.

35. Ibid.

36. Hershey, "U.S. Jobless," 30.

37. Coontz, *The Way,* 264.

38. *The State of America's Children Yearbook 1996,* 6.

39. Timmer, Eitzen, and Talley, *The Path*, 25.

40. Ibid., 25, 84.

41. MacDermid and Targ, "A Call For," 159.

42. Barry Bluestone, Bennett Harrison, and Lucy Gorham, "Storm

Clouds on the Horizon: Labor Market Crisis and Industrial Policy," *Dollars and Sense* 115 (1986): 6.

43. MacDermid and Targ, "A Call For," 155.

44. Coontz, *The Way*, 234.

45. Ibid., 233.

46. Kathryn M. Neckerman and Joleen Kirschenman, "Hiring Strategies, Racial Bias, and Inner-City Workers." *Social Problems* 38 (1991): 433–47.

47. Coontz, *The Way*, 234.

48. Ibid., 251; William J. Wilson with Kathryn Neckerman, "Poverty and Family Structure: The Widening Gap between Evidence and Public Policy Issues," in *The Truly Disadvantaged: The Inner City, the Underclass, and Public Policy*, by William J. Wilson (Chicago: University of Chicago Press, 1987).

49. Cliff Johnson and Andrew Sum, *Declining Earnings of Young Men: Their Relationship to Poverty, Teen Pregnancy, and Family Formation* (Washington, D.C.: Adolescent Pregnancy Prevention Clearing House, 1987).

50. Coontz, *The Way* 252.

51. Wilson, *The Truly Disadvantaged*, 145–56.

52. Haya Stier and Marta Tienda, "Are Men Marginal to The Family?: Insights from Chicago's Inner City," in *Men, Work, and Family*, edited by Jane C. Hood (Newbury Park, Calif.: Sage, 1995), 33.

53. Wilson, *The Truly Disadvantaged*, 60–61, 158.

54. Ellen L. Bassuk, "Social and Economic Hardships of Homeless and Other Poor Women," *American Journal of Orthopsychiatry* 63 (1993): 340–47.

55. Diana Pearce, "The Feminization of Poverty: Update," in *Feminist Frontiers*, edited by Alison M. Jagger and Paula S. Rothenberg (New York: McGraw-Hill, 1989), 290.

56. Coontz, *The Way*, 4.

57. Lynne M. Casper, Sara S. McLanahan, and Irwin Garfinkel, "The Gender-Poverty Gap: What We Can Learn from Other Countries," *American Sociological Review* 59 (1994): 598.

58. Andrew Cherlin, *Marriage, Divorce, Remarriage* (Cambridge: Harvard University Press, 1981), 81.

59. Pearce, "The Feminization," 291.

60. Coontz, *The Way,* 260; Laurence Mischel and David Frankel, *The*

State of Working America 1990-1991 Edition. (Armonk, N.Y.: M. E. Sharpe, 1991), 6.

61. Coontz, *The Way,* 259.

62. Ibid., 251.

63. Kathryn Edin, "Surviving the Welfare System: How AFDC Recipients Make Ends Meet in Chicago," *Social Problems* 4 (1991): 471.

64. Ibid.

65. Richard B. Freeman, *Working under Different Rules* New York: Russell Sage Foundation, 1994), 177.

66. Ibid., 178.

CHAPTER 3

1. Michael Sosin, "Homeless and Vulnerable Meal Program Users: A Comparison Study," *Social Problems* 39 (1992): 171.

2. Ibid.

3. David Wagner and Marcia B. Cohen, "The Power of the People: Homeless Protesters in the Aftermath of Social Movement Participation," *Social Problems* 38 (1991): 544.

4. Margaret B. Wilkerson and Jewell Handy Gresham, "The Racialization of Poverty," in *Feminist Frameworks,* edited by Alison Jagger and Paula S. Rothenberg (New York: McGraw-Hill, 1993) 301.

5. Goffman, *Asylum.*

6. Timmer, Eitzen, and Talley, *Paths,* 106.

7. Goffman, *Asylum.*

8. Timmer, Eitzen, and Talley. *Paths*, 106.

9. Robert Perucci, *Circle of Madness,* (Englewood Cliffs, N.J.: Prentice Hall, 1974).

10. Bonnie Hausman and Constance Hammen, "Parenting in Homeless Families: The Double Crisis," *American Journal of Orthopsychiatry* 63 (1993): 360.

CHAPTER 4

1. Lineham, "Children Who Are Homeless," 62–63.

2. E. Anne Eddowes, "Schools Providing Safer Environments for Homeless Children," *Childhood Education* (1994): 271–72.

3. Ibid.

4. Kathleen J. Moroz and Elizabeth A. Segal, "Homeless Children: Intervention Strategies for School Social Workers," *Social Work in Education* 12 (1990): 136.

5. Jewell Taylor Gibbs, "Assessment of Depression in Urban Adolescent Females: Implications for Early Intervention Strategies," *American Journal of Social Psychiatry* 6 (1986): 50–56; Jane D. McLeod and Michael J. Shanahan, "Poverty, Parenting, and Children's Mental Health," *American Sociological Review* 58 (1993): 351–66.

6. Moroz and Segal, "Homeless Children," 134, 136; Linehan, "Children Who," 62; *The State of America's Children 1992*, 38–39.

7. Eddowes, "Schools Providing," 271–72.

8. Ibid.

9. P. L. Maza and J. A. Hall, *Homeless Children and Their Families: A Preliminary Study* (Washington, D.C.: Child Welfare League of America, 1988), 120.

10. Pierre Bordieu, *Reproduction in Education, Society, and Culture* (London: Sage, 1990), 11–19.

11. *The State of America's Children Yearbook 1996*, 39.

12. Bordieu, *Reproduction in Education,* 21.

13. Martina Morris, Annette D. Berhnhardt, and Mark S. Handcock. "Economic Inequality: New Methods for New Trends," *American Sociological Review* (1994) 59: 205–19.

14. Jeanne Brooks-Gunn, Greg J. Duncan, Pamela Kato Klevanov, and Naomi Sealand, "Do Neighborhoods Influence Child and Adolescent Development?" *American Journal of Sociology* 99 (1993): 353–95; Jonathan Crane, "Effects of Neighborhoods on Dropping Out of School and Teenage Childbearing," in *The Urban Underclass*, edited by Christopher Jencks and Paul E. Peterson (Washington, D.C.: Brookings Institute, 1991), 299–320.

15. *The State of America's Children 1992*.

16. Linehan, "Children Who," 63.

17. Charles Cooley, *Human Nature and the Social Order* (New York: Schocken, 1964).

18. Shelley Koblinsky and Elaine A. Anderson, "Serving Homeless Children and Families in Head Start," *Children Today* 22 (1993): 20; Linehan, "Children Who," 62; Linda J. Stevens and Marianne Price, "Meeting the Challenge of Educating Children at Risk," *Phi Delta Kappan* (September 1992): 19.

19. Mills and Ota, "Homeless Women," 488.

20. Phillipe Aries, *Centuries of Childhood: A Social History of Family Life* (New York: Random House, 1962).

21. Linda Weinrab and John C. Buckner, "Homeless Families: Program Responses and Public Policies," *American Journal of Orthopsychiatry* 63 (1993): 401.

CHAPTER 5

1. "The Kentucky Family and Children's Initiative, Fiscal Year 1996, Application Guidelines" (Frankfort, Kentucky: Commission on Families and Children, March 1995), 1–4.

2. Lindblom, "Toward a Comprehensive," 974.

3. Ibid., 968.

CHAPTER 6

1. John F. Longres and Eileen McLeod, "Consciousness Raising and Social Work Practice," *The Journal of Contemporary Social Work* 61 (1980): 268.

2. Wagner and Cohen, "The Power of the People," 555.

3. Cooley, *Human Nature.*

4. Mills, *Sociological Imagination.*

5. Dorothy Smith, *The Everyday World as Problematic* (Boston: Northeastern University Press, 1987), 34–36.

6. Paulo Freire, *Pedagogy of the Oppressed* (New York: Seabury Press, 1970); Longres and McLeod, "Consciousness Raising," 267.

7. Patricia Hill Collins, "The Social Construction of Black Feminist Thought," in *Feminist Frontiers III*, edited by Laurel Richardson and Verta Taylor (New York: McGraw Hill, 1993), 220.

8. Geneva Smitherman, *Talkin and Tesifyin: The Language of Black America* (Detroit: Wayne State University Press, 1986), 76.

CHAPTER 7

1. Coontz, *The Way*, 286–87.

2. Ibid., 76–79.

3. MacDermid and Targ, "A Call For," 155.

4. Karin Sandqvist, "Sweden's Sex-Role Scheme and Commitment to Gender Equality," in *Dual-Earner Families: International Perspectives,* edited by Suzan Lewis, Dafna N. Ezraeli, and Helen Hootsman (London: Sage, 1992), 81–82.

5. Lindblom, "Toward a Comprehensive," 992.

6. Michael Winerip, "Doors Shut to Poor Seeking Homes: Since Federal Cuts, Landlords Abandon Rent-Subsidy Programs," *New York Times,*

July 22, 1996, A 6.

7. Lindblom, "Toward a Comprehensive," 987.

8. Winerip, "Doors Shut," A 6.

9. Lindblom, "Toward a Comprehensive," 994–95.

10. Ibid., 997.

11. Stephen L. Nock and Paul W. Kingston, *The Sociology of Public Issues* (Belmont, Calif.: Wadsworth, 1990), 80.

12. Alice Kessler-Harris, "The Wage Conceived: Value and Need as Measures of a Woman's Worth," in *Feminist Frontiers III,* edited by Laurel Richardson and Verta Taylor (New York: McGraw Hill, 1993), 184–85, 187.

13. MacDermid and Targ, "A Call," 159.

14. Barrie Thorne, "Feminism and the Family," in *Rethinking the Family: Some Feminist Questions*, edited by Barrie Thorne and Marilyn Yalom (Boston: Northeastern University Press, 1992), 11.

15. *The State of America's Children 1992*, 19.

16. *The State of America's Children Yearbook 1996*, 30.

17. Ibid.

EPILOGUE

1. Mills, *Sociological Imagination.*

2. Popenoe, "American Family," 527–42.

3. Arlene Skolnick, *Embattled Paradise* (New York: Basic Books, 1991).

4. Naomi Wolf, *The Beauty Myth: How Images of Beauty Are Used against Women.* (New York: Anchor Books, 1991).

5. Peter T. Kilborn and Sam Howe Verhover, "Clinton's Shift on Welfare Bill Reflects Vision as a New Democrat," *New York Times,* August 2, 1996, A 8.

6. Ibid.

7. Clifford J. Levy, "Pataki May Call Special Legislative Session to Cope with Impact of U.S. Welfare Bill," *New York Times*, August 2, 1996, A 9.

8. Michael Janofsky, "Welfare Cuts Raise Fears for Mayors," *New York Times*, July 30, 1996, C 20.

9. Katherine Newman, "Working Poor, Working Hard," *The Nation,* July 29/August 5, 1996, 20–23.

10. Katha Pollitt, "Utopia, Limited," *The Nation,* July 29/August 5, 1996, 9.

Bibliography

Aries, Phillip. 1962. *Centuries of Childhood: A Social History of Family Life*. New York: Random House.

Bachrach, Leona L. 1987. "Homeless Women: A Context for Health Planning." *The Milbank Quarterly* 65: 371–96.

Bassuk, Ellen L. 1993. "Social and Economic Hardships of Homeless and Other Poor Women." *American Journal of Orthopsychiatry* 63: 340–47.

Baum, Alice S., and Donald W. Burnes. 1993. *A Nation in Denial: The Truth about Homelessness*. Boulder: Westview Press.

Berger, Peter L., and Thomas Luckmann. 1966. *The Social Construction of Reality*. New York: Doubleday.

Blankenhorn, David. 1990. "Does Grandmother Know Best?" *Family Affairs* 3: 13–16.

Bluestone, Barry, Bennett Harrison, and Lucy Gorham. 1986. "Storm Clouds on the Horizon: Labor Market Crisis and Industrial Policy." *Dollars and Sense* 115: 6.

Brooks-Gunn, Jeanne, Greg J. Duncan, Pamela Kato Klevanov, and Naomi Sealand. 1993. "Do Neighborhoods Influence Child and Adolescent Development?" *American Journal of Sociology* 99: 353–95.

Bordieu, Pierre. 1990. *Reproduction in Education, Society, and Culture*. London: Sage.

Burt, Martha. 1992. *Over the Edge: The Growth of Homelessness in the 1980s*. New York: Russell Sage Foundation.

Casper, Lynn M., Sara S. McLanahan, and Irwin Garfinkel. 1994. "The Gender-Poverty Gap: What We Can Learn from Other Countries." *American Sociological Review* 59: 594–605.

Cherlin, Andrew. 1981. *Marriage, Divorce, Remarriage*. Cambridge: Harvard University Press.

Collins, Patricia Hill. 1993. "The Social Construction of Black Feminist Thought." 20–29. In *Feminist Frontiers III*, edited by Laurel Richardson and Verta Taylor, New York: McGraw-Hill.

Cooley, Charles. 1964. *Human Nature and the Social Order*. New York: Schocken.

Coontz, Stephanie. 1992. *The Way We Never Were: American Families and the Nostalgia Trap*. New York: Basic Books.

Crane, Jonathan. 1991. "Effects of Neighborhoods on Dropping Out of School and Teenage Childbearing." 229–320. In *The Urban Underclass*, edited by Christopher Jencks and Paul E. Peterson. Washington, D.C.: Brookings Institute.

Duncan, Greg J., and Willard Rodgers. 1991. "Has Children's Poverty Become More Persistent?" *American Sociological Review* 56: 538–50.

Dupper, David R., and Anthony P. Halter. 1994. "Barriers in Educating Children from Homeless Shelters: Perspectives of School and Shelter Staff." *Social Work in Education* 16: 39–45.

Eddowes, E. Anne. 1994. "Schools Providing Safer Environments for Homeless Children." *Childhood Education* (Annual Theme): 271–73.

Edin, Kathryn. 1991. "Surviving the Welfare System: How AFDC Recipients Make Ends Meet in Chicago." *Social Problems* 4: 462–74.

Eitzen, Stanley, and Maxine Baca Zinn. 1993. *In Conflict and Order: Understanding Society*. Boston: Allyn and Bacon.

Ellington, George. 1869. *The Women of New York*. New York: New York Books.

Elliott, Marta and Lauren J. Krivo. 1991. "Structural Determinants of Homelessness in the United States." *Social Problems* 38: 113–31.

"The Flap over Executive Pay." 1991/1994. *Business Week* (May 6, 1991); reprinted in *Sociology: Windows on Society* (1994), edited by John W. Heeren and Marylee Mason. Los Angeles: Roxbury.

Freeman, Richard B. 1994. *Working under Different Rules*. New York: Russell Sage Foundation.

Freire, Paulo. 1970. *Pedagogy of the Oppressed*. New York: Seabury Press.

Gibbs, Jewell Taylor. 1986. "Assessment of Depression in Urban Adolescent Females: Implications for Early Intervention Strategies." *American Journal of Social Psychiatry* 6: 50–56.

Goffman, Erving. 1961. *Asylum*. Garden City, N.Y.: Anchor Books.

———. 1963. *Stigma: Notes on the Management of Spoiled Identity*. Englewood Cliffs, N.J.: Prentice Hall.

Golden, Stephanie. 1992. *The Women Outside: Meanings and Myths of Homelessness*. Berkeley: University of California Press.

Harris, Mullan Kathleen. 1996. "Life after Welfare: Women, Work, and Repeat Dependency." *American Sociological Review* 61: 407–26.

Hartman, Chester. 1974. *Yerba Buena: Land Grab and Community Resistance in San Francisco*. San Francisco: Glide Publications.

Hausman, Bonnie, and Constance Hammen. 1993. "Parenting in Homeless Families: The Double Crisis." *American Journal of Orthopsychiatry* 63: 358–69.

Head, Simon. 1996. "The New, Ruthless Economy." *The New York Review of Books* (February 26): 47–52.

Hershey, Robert D., Jr. 1996. "Thesis: Wage Rise Will Hurt Teenagers." *New York Times* (July 9): C 6.

Hochschild, Arlie. 1989. *The Second Shift*. New York: Viking.

Janofsky, Michael. 1996. "Welfare Cuts Raise Fears for Mayors." *New York Times* (July 30): C 20.

Johnson, Cliff, and Andrew Sum. 1987. *Declining Earnings of Young Men: Their Relationship to Poverty, Teen Pregnancy, and Family Formation*. Washington, D.C.: Adolescent Pregnancy Prevention Clearing House.

"The Kentucky Family and Children's Initiative, Fiscal Year 1996: Application Guidelines." 1995. Frankfort, Ky.: Commission on Families and Children (March).

Kessler-Harris, Alice. 1993. "The Wage Conceived: Value and Need as Measures of a Woman's Worth." 183–97. In *Feminist Frontiers III*, edited by Laurel Richardson and Verta Taylor. New York: McGraw Hill.

Kilborn, Peter T., and Sam Howe Verhover. 1996. "Clinton's Shift on Welfare Bill Reflects Vision as a New Democrat." *New York Times* (August 2): A 8.

Koblinsky, Shelley, and Elaine A. Anderson. 1993. "Serving Homeless Children and Families in Head Start." *Children Today* 22: 19–36.

Kozol, Jonathan. 1988. *Rachel and Her Children: Homeless Families in America.* New York: Fawcett Columbine.

Levy, Clifford J. 1996. "Pataki May Call Special Legislative Session to Cope with Impact of U.S. Welfare Bill." *New York Times* (August 2): A 9.

Lindblom, Eric. 1991. "Toward a Comprehensive Homelessness Prevention Strategy." *Housing Policy Debate 2*: 957–1025.

Linehan, Michelle Fryt. 1992. "Children Who Are Homeless: Educational Strategies." *Phi Delta Kappan* (September): 61–64.

Longres, John F., and Eileen McLeod. 1980. "Consciousness Raising and Social Work Practice." *The Journal of Contemporary Social Work* 61: 267–76.

MacDermid, Shelley M. and Dena B. Targ. 1995. "A Call for Greater Attention to the Role of Employers in Developing, Transforming, and Implementing Family Policies." *Journal of Family and Economic Studies* 16: 145–70.

Maza, P. L., and J. A. Hall. 1988. *Homeless Children and Their Families: A Preliminary Study.* Washington, D.C.: Child Welfare League of America.

McLeod, Jane D., and Michael J. Shanahan. 1993. "Poverty, Parenting, and Children's Mental Health." *American Sociological Review* 58: 351–66.

Miller, Kathy. 1996. "Work, Family, and the Good Provider Role: Factors Affecting Rural and Farm Women's Work in Indiana from 1900–1958." Paper presented at the North Central Sociological Association Conference, Cincinnati, Ohio, April 13, 1996.

Mills, Crystal, and Hiro Ota. 1989. "Homeless Women with Minor Children in the Detroit Metropolitan Area." *Social Work* (November): 485–89.

Mischel, Laurence, and David Frankel. 1991. *The State of Working America, 1990–1991 Edition.* Armonk, N.Y.: M.E. Sharpe.

Moore, Thomas A. 1996. *The Disposable Work Force: Worker Displacement and Employment Instability in America.* Hawthorne, N.Y.: Aldine Deupree Gruyter

Moroz, Kathleen J., and Elizabeth A. Segal. 1990. "Homeless Children: Intervention Strategies for School Social Workers." *Social Work in Education* 12: 134–43.

Morris, Martina, Annette D. Bernhardt, and Mark S. Handcock. 1994. "Economic Inequality: New Methods for New Trends." *American Sociological Review* 59: 205–19.

Neckerman, Kathryn M., and Joleen Kirschenman. 1991. "Hiring Strate gies, Racial Bias, and Inner-City Workers." *Social Problems* 38: 433–47.

Newman, Katherine. 1996. "Working Poor, Working Hard." *The Nation* (July 29/August 6): 20–23.

Nock, Stephen L., and Paul W. Kingston. 1990. *The Sociology of Public Issues.* Belmont, Calif.: Wadsworth.

Pearce, Diana. 1989. "The Feminization of Poverty: Update," 290–96. In *Feminist Frameworks,* edited by Alison M. Jagger and Paula S. Rothenberg. New York: McGraw-Hill.

Perucci, Robert. 1974. *Circle of Madness.* Englewood Cliffs, N. J.: Prentice Hall.

Pollitt, Katha. 1996. "Utopia, Limited." *The Nation* (July 29/August 5):9.

Popenoe, David. 1993. "American Family Decline, 1960–1990: A Review and Appraisal." *Journal of Marriage and the Family* 55: 527–42.

Reich, Robert B. 1991. *The Work of Nations.* New York: Vintage.

Rossi, Peter. 1989. *Down and Out in America: The Origins of Homelessness.* Chicago: University of Chicago Press.

Sandqvist, Karin. 1992. "Sweden's Sex-Role Scheme and Commitment to Gender Equality," 80–98. In *Dual-Earner Families: International Perspectives*, edited by Suzan Lewis, Dafna N. Ezraeli, and Helen Hootsman. London: Sage.

Skolnick, Arlene. 1991. *Embattled Paradise.* New York: Basic Books.

Smith, Dorothy. 1987. *The Everyday World as Problematic.* Boston: Northeastern University Press.

Smitherman, Geneva. 1986. *Talkin and Testifyin: The Language of Black America.* Detroit: Wayne State University Press.

Sosin, Michael. 1992. "Homeless and Vulnerable Meal Program Users: A Comparison Study." *Social Problems* 39: 170–88.

Stacey, Judith. 1992. "Backward toward the Postmodern Family: Reflections on Gender, Kinship, and Class in the Silicon Valley," 91–118. In *Rethinking the Family: Some Feminist Questions,* edited by Barrie Thorne and Marilyn Yalom. Boston: Northeastern University Press.

————. 1994. "Dan Quayle's Revenge: The New Family Values Crusaders." *The Nation* (July 25/August 1): 119–22. (March).

The State of America's Children 1992. Washington, D.C.: Children's Defense Fund.

The State of America's Children Yearbook 1996. Washington, D.C.: Children's Defense Fund.

Stefl, Mary E. 1987. "The New Homeless: A National Perspective," 44–63. In *Homeless in Contemporary Society*, edited by Richard D. Bingham, Roy E. Green, and Sammis B. White. Newbury Park, Calif: Sage.

Stevens, Linda J., and Marianne Price. 1992. "Meeting the Challenge of Educating Children at Risk." *Phi Delta Kappan* (September): 18–23.

Stier, Haya, and Marta Tienda. 1995. "Are Men Marginal to the Family? Insights from Chicago's Inner City," 23–44. In *Men, Work, and Family*, edited by Jane C. Hood, Newbury Park, Calif.: Sage.

Thorne, Barrie. 1992. "Feminism and the Family," 3–30. In *Rethinking the Family: Some Feminist Questions*, edited by Barrie Thorne and Marilyn Yalom. Boston: Northeastern University Press.

Timmer, Doug A., D. Stanley Eitzen, and Kathryn D. Talley. 1994. *Paths to Homelessness: Extreme Poverty and the Urban Housing Crisis*. Boulder: Westview Press.

Wagner, David, and Marcia B. Cohen. 1991. "The Power of the People: Homeless Protesters in the Aftermath of Social Movement Participation." *Social Problems* 38: 543–61.

Weiner, Lynn Y. 1985. *From Working Girl to Working Mother: The Female Labor Force in the United States, 1820–1980*. Chapel Hill: University of North Carolina Press.

Weinrab, Linda, and John C. Buckner. 1993. "Homeless Families: Program Responses and Public Policies." *American Journal of Orthopsychiatry* 63: 400–8.

Wilkerson, Margaret B. and Jewell Handy Gresham. 1993. "The Racialization of Poverty," 297–303. In *Feminist Frameworks*, edited by Alison Jagger and Paula S. Rothenberg. New York: McGraw-Hill.

Wilson, William J. 1987. *The Truly Disadvantaged: The Inner City, the Underclass, and Public Policy*. Chicago: University of Chicago Press.

Winerip, Michael. 1996. "Doors Shut to Poor Seeking Homes: Since Federal Cuts, Landlords Abandon Rent-Subsidy Programs." *New York Times* (July 22): A 6.

Wolf, Naomi. 1991. *The Beauty Myth: How Images of Beauty Are Used against Women*. New York: Anchor Books.

Index

About the Author

BARBARA A. ARRIGHI is Assistant Professor of Sociology at Northern Kentucky University. Her articles have been published in professional journals and in the *Encyclopedia of Marriage and the Family.*